Is That You, Lord?

IS THAT
YOU
LORD?

HEARING THE
VOICE OF THE LORD

A BIBLICAL PERSPECTIVE

Dr Gary E. Gilley

EVANGELICAL PRESS

EVANGELICAL PRESS

Evangelical Press
Faverdale North Industrial Estate, Darlington, DL3 0PH England
email: sales@evangelicalpress.org

Evangelical Press USA
PO Box 825, Webster, NY 14580 USA
email: usa.sales@evangelicalpress.org

www.evangelicalpress.org

First published 2007

Printed in the United States of America

British Library Cataloguing in Publication Data available

ISBN-13 978 0 85234 625 5

CONTENTS

They who leave the light of the Word
and follow the light within them,
as some say, prefer the shining of the
glow-worm before the sun.

Thomas Watson

This book is dedicated to my sons, Benjamin and
Brian. What joy it brings me to know that you both
walk with the Lord and seek to serve him.

FOREWORD

I would like to call this book a welcome addition to the plethora of scholarly works that uncover the theological error of 'continuing revelation'. However, such a collection of books is not available that responds exhaustively to the view of inerrant and extra-biblical, divine knowledge of God's perfect will. Such works are usually rare, complex and unread by the average saint. Of course, many conservative evangelicals and fundamentalists have written to contest the open canon views of the Roman church, cults and charismatics. The conclusion in many of these works is that God is not speaking to these other groups but somehow he does speak to evangelicals. Thus, many evangelicals strongly contend for the inerrancy of Scripture without embracing the *sole authority* and *all sufficiency* which Scripture claims for itself.

Gary Gilley has not produced a superficial revision of other works on this subject. On the contrary, his direct writing style has reduced an extremely complex subject to easily digestible bites that will become powerful tools in the hands of the average Christian. The reader, in addition to becoming familiarized with the historical roots of pietism, subjectivism and the mysticism that affects much thinking today, will become thoroughly enmeshed in the biblical reasons why further revelation from God is unnecessary today. Christ's promise that the Spirit would grant total recall and personal inerrancy was directed only to the men who would deliver the doctrines of the New Testament church for the dispensation of grace. These truths have been handed down to us within the pages of a closed canon of Scripture.

From James 4:13-16 the reader discovers that he must not boast of divine knowledge of his personal and geographic destiny because no one knows from God whether he will still be living by this time tomorrow. How unfruitful it is to spend time listening for the voice of God when you could spend intimate time in confession and prayer and the reading of God's complete message in the Bible.

The reader will learn that there are no inerrant impressions or convictions from the Holy Spirit that are not at the same time clear biblical precepts. In Psalm 37:23 the Psalmist says that 'the steps of a good man are ordered by the Lord' and then qualifies himself in 119:133 by saying 'order my steps in thy Word'. In 119:105 the 'Word is a lamp unto my feet, and a light unto my path'. For Gary Gilley, the Word does not need light — it is light. Satan himself knows this full well since he has 'blinded the minds of them which believe not, lest the light of the glorious gospel of Christ, who is the image of God, should shine unto them' (2 Cor. 4:4).

To those who would contend that Dr Gilley's view is dead and lifeless and carries no impact on the life of the believer, we will let God respond: 'Is not my word like as a fire? saith the Lord; and like a hammer that breaketh the rock in pieces' (Jer. 23:29)?

Gary Gilley's position on this subject is in agreement with the first generation of pastors following the apostolic period. Polycarp was the disciple of the Apostle John and in turn mentored Irenaeus who, in his third book against heresies, said:

> It is within the power of all, therefore, in every Church, who may wish to see the truth, to contemplate clearly the tradition of the apostles manifested throughout the whole world; and we are in a position to reckon up those who were by the apostles instituted bishops in the Churches, and [to demonstrate] the succession of these men to our own times; those who neither taught nor knew of anything like what these [heretics] rave about. For if the apostles had known hidden mysteries, which they were in the habit of imparting to 'the

perfect' apart and privily from the rest, they would
have delivered them especially to those to whom they
were also committing the churches themselves (Book
III, Chap. iii.3).

In Book III, Chap. iii.3 Irenaeus gives the history of the first
twelve pastors of the church at Rome and then states: 'And this
is most abundant proof that there is one and the same vivifying
faith, which has been preserved in the Church from the Apostles
until now, and handed down in truth.'

Irenaeus learned the *sole authority of the apostolic tradition*
[what Gary Gilley would refer to as the 'sole authority of the
Scriptures'] from none other than Polycarp when he wrote:

But Polycarp also was not only instructed by apostles,
and conversed with many who had seen Christ, but
was also, by apostles in Asia, appointed bishop of the
Church in Smyrna, whom I also saw in my early youth,
for he tarried [on earth] a very long time, and when a
very old man, gloriously and most nobly suffering mar-
tyrdom, departed this life, having always taught the
things which he had learned from the apostles, and
which the Church has handed down, and which alone
are true. To these things the Asiatic Churches testify,
as do also those men who have succeeded Polycarp
down to the present time, — a man who was of much
greater weight, and a more steadfast witness of the
truth than Valentinus, and Marcion, and the rest of the
heretics. He it was who, coming to Rome in the time
of Anicetus, caused many to turn away from the afore-
said heretics to the Church of God, proclaiming that
he had received this one and sole truth from the apostles... (Book III, Chap. iii.4).

Let this book teach us what Irenaeus knew — namely that
New Testament truth from God is a closed system to which nothing can be added and is present with us today in the Scriptures
alone. Irenaeus said,

Since, therefore, the tradition from the apostles does thus exist in the Church, and is permanent among us, let us revert to the Scriptural proof furnished by those apostles who did also write the Gospel, in which they recorded the doctrine regarding God, pointing out that our Lord Jesus Christ is the truth, and that no lie is in him (Book III, Chap. v.1).

Let the reader ponder the arguments of this research and weigh them with an open Bible. Those of us who have found complete satisfaction in God's revelation through the Holy Scriptures have long awaited a book like this. We can be expected to distribute multiple copies to our friends and colleagues in order that they also may catch the challenge of this issue.

Dr John O. Hosler, Senior Pastor
Napier Parkview Baptist Church
Benton Harbor, Michigan

INTRODUCTION

Communication, in this modern age of communication, can be frustrating on many levels. Consider the common cell phone. Many nimbly leap from phone call to text message to taking a picture of a friend, all with the efficiency of a technological Jedi. Others, mortally fearful of missing a call, trot around with a 'Bluetooth' attached to their ear (my regular jest to such people, that they have 'a little something in their ear' has so far failed to elicit a chuckle). Such people have mastered the art of modern communication, at least of this variety.

Then there are the technologically challenged. Our one-year-old grandson has a better chance of activating the television through use of the remote than many a middle-aged adult has. When it comes to the cell phone it gets worse. Everyone seems to have a cell phone these days but legions are totally perplexed as to how to go about retrieving messages. How frustrated they are to see the little screen indicating they have a message but have no concept of how to retrieve it.

Perhaps this is how many of us feel about messages from God. It wasn't so bad when we were using the old communication technique — you know, the Bible. Back when we were taught that prayer was us speaking to God and Scripture was God speaking to us. We understood at that time how such communication from the Lord worked. We read and studied the Word to understand God and his instructions for living. This was not always easy, but with careful effort and proper technique we had a handle on God's instructions. Then along came new and 'improved' methods. We were told that God had a specific will for each of our lives and, more importantly, we had to find it. We were now on a celestial treasure hunt to 'discover the will of God'. Complicating matters further was that the Bible provided no instructions to aid in this search. Instead, we were told that the Lord was providing a sort of new and fresh revelation completely apart from biblical revelation. It was personalized revelation directed specifically at each individual. It was the voice of God but not audibly heard. This voice was an inner voice most likely detected through hunches, feelings, promptings and circumstances. And adding to the gravity of the situation was the warning that to miss this voice, or even misinterpret it, would doom us to living outside the will of God — perhaps for life.

An array of books, seminars and sermons was developed to instruct and train concerned Christians to 'retrieve' these messages from God. However, the instruction manuals, having not been written by God, tended towards conjecture and guesswork, were often contradictory and left the weary believer apprehensive at best. How do I know, they often asked, if I am really hearing the voice of God? Could it be my own imagination or desires? Could it be the suggestions of others or even the devil at play? Could it be that pepperoni pizza I ate at midnight?

Like many frantically searching through a series of instructions hoping to unlock the secret to the latest message from a friend, the child of God fished through the plethora of man-made instructions to discover God's messages. But here the stakes are higher. My wife may have missed my message to bring home ice cream, but the believer fears that he may have missed God's message concerning a spouse, a career change, what church to attend or automobile to purchase.

It is for such frustrated and perplexed people that I have written this book. It is my hope that these thoughts will help unravel some of the confusion. In this book I would like to press home the great need of the hour: the need for confidence in the Word, the only authoritative voice of God for all ages. Ruth Tucker frames my quest well in *God Talk*:

> No one would deny that the Bible provides examples of God speaking. That is not the issue. Rather, the debate centers on when and how and why God spoke, and whether that kind of

speaking continues on after the completion of the biblical canon. An important issue is whether God spoke to ordinary folks in biblical times on a routine basis.[1]

The answers to these questions, as I understand them, are found in the pages that follow.

CHAPTER 1

PIETISM AND SUBJECTIVE CHRISTIANITY

Balance. Is there anything more elusive? Most of us are constantly striving for balance, whether it is with our time, money, diet or relationships. If few of us are ever content that we have found just the right balance in these areas of life, the same can be said for the historical church. God's people tend to swing from one extreme to another with great regularity, causing considerable tension within the body of Christ. One such tension has been, and still is, between the academic and the experiential, between those who place great emphasis on the theological and those who place the bulk of their emphasis on the subjective. Subjective oriented believers cast the term 'dead orthodoxy' at their counterpart. I vividly remember an extremist group marching around the walls of Moody Bible Institute when I was a student there, crying out, 'Babylon is falling down'. This same group purposely mispronounced 'seminary' (calling it cemetery) and loved quoting 2 Corinthians 3:6b, 'For the letter kills, but the Spirit gives life.'

Doctrinally-inclined Christians cast aspersions such as 'heterodox' at such people (you have to be doctrinally inclined to cast such aspersions). The proper biblical balance is for theology to result in doxology, and doxology to lead to holy, passionate living for Jesus Christ. Unfortunately it seldom seems to be that easy, and so the tension between theology and experience goes on and the balance hard to find. This is a modern day struggle but it has much historical precedent. One such precedent, which still has major ramifications for us today, has been termed 'Pietism'.

A Little History

Pietism began as a reaction to the highly intellectualized orthodoxy that had become common in Lutheran and Reformed churches in the decades following the Reformation.

> Pietism made its appearance as a distinct historical movement within Protestantism, at the end of the seventeenth and beginning of the eighteenth centuries, around 1690-1730. Its aim was to stress 'practical piety', as distinct from the polemical dogmatic theology to which the Reformation had initially given a certain priority. Against the intellectualist and abstract understanding of God and of dogmatic truth, pietism set a practical, active piety (praxis pietatis): good works, daily self-examination for progress in virtues according to objective criteria, daily study of the Bible and practical application of its moral teaching, intense emotionalism in prayer, a clear break with the 'world' and worldly practices (dancing, the theatre, non-religious reading); and tendencies towards separatism, with the movement holding private meetings and distinguishing itself from the 'official Church'.[1]

While there have been many leaders among the Pietists, most recognize the big four as follows:

Johann Arndt (1555-1621). He is considered by modern historians to be the 'Father of Pietism'. Arndt's most lasting influence came through his six-volume devotional work *True Christianity* (1606). This was a collection of sermons which relied heavily on the mystics, especially Thomas à Kempis. Arndt was not a classical mystic but he was concerned, especially in book three, with how one could find the Kingdom of God within oneself. His answer was found in self-denial as opposed to intellectual pursuit.

Arndt, in reaction to what he considered the dead-orthodoxy of Lutheranism, preached that the evidence of conversion was not correct doctrine but a changed life.

Philip Jacob Spener (1635-1705). Spener wrote his major work *Pia Desideria* (*Pious Desires*), subtitled *Heartfelt Desire for God-Pleasing Reform*, in 1675. Many Lutherans date the beginning of Pietism with the publication of this book, which became a manual of Pietistic reforms. Spener, taking Arndt one step further, more aggressively combated those who promoted doctrine to the neglect of piety. Spener did not minimize Scripture but there was a subtle almost indiscernible shift towards experience

Auguste Hermann Francke (1663-1727). As Spener's successor, Francke continued and expanded Spener's emphasis on a changed life and practical theology. He was known for his kindness and great interest in foreign missions, as well as his ecumenical spirit.

Count Nicolaus Ludwig Von Zinzendorf (1700-1760). In Zinzendorf the teachings of Arndt, Spener and Francke bear their natural fruit. Zinzendorf developed a system he called 'Theology of the Heart', which basically meant that heart-felt religious convictions and experiences were more trustworthy than theological understanding. As a natural outworking of this philosophy Zinzendorf emphasized the ecumenism of Francke, teaching that doctrinal difference between believers should be tolerated. Zinzendorf is best known today because of his leadership within the Moravians, a Pietist sect that had profound impact on the life of John Wesley.

What Did Pietism Teach?

While Pietism had its original roots in Lutheranism, historians identify at least three other branches of early Pietism including Reformed, Moravian and Radical.[2] It is therefore difficult to pin down the exact beliefs of the Pietists, but there were some definite common threads that can be traced throughout all of these branches.

Spener offered six proposals for reform in *Pia Desideria*, which became a short summary of Pietism:

- There should be 'a more extensive use of the Word of God among us'. 'The Bible', Spener said, 'must be the chief means for reforming something'.

- Spener called also for a renewal of 'the spiritual priesthood', the priesthood of all believers. Here he cited Luther's example in urging all Christians to be active in the general work of Christian ministry.

- He appealed for the reality of Christian practice and argued that Christianity is more than a matter of simple knowledge.

- Spener then urged restraint and charity in religious controversies. He asked his readers to love and pray for unbelievers and the erring, and to adopt a moderate tone in disputes.

- Next he called for a reform in the education of ministers. Here he stressed the need for training in piety and devotion as well as in academic subjects.

- Last he implored ministers to preach edifying sermons, understandable by the people, rather than technical discourses which few were interested in or could understand.[3]

On the surface there seems little to object in Spener's proposals; but while he had a concern for proper exegesis, and a high regard for the Bible, he and other Pietists were slowly allowing experience and subjectivism to become more authoritative than Scripture. By the time we get to Zinzendorf this exchange had become obvious. Experience, despite what might be officially stated, had in practice become the final arbitrator in the lives of the Moravians. 'Zinzendorf stressed the importance of experiencing God',[4] to the extent of allowing for personal experience to determine the meaning of Scripture and frame Christian living. Based upon the studies of J. E. Hutton, historian of the Moravian movement, Arnold Dallimore writes:

> To them the value of the Bible consisted, not in its supposed infallibility, but in its appeal to their hearts... The Bible was not its supreme authority, but authority lay also in personal experience, and, of course, varied according to the sentiments of the individual. Nor was the Bible a book to which they gave diligent study; they regarded it somewhat as a compilation of texts and mottoes, and they had the curious practice of opening it at random and accepting the first verse their eye lighted upon as the immediate guidance of heaven. They employed it also in the casting of lots and we are told that the Count 'carried his lot apparatus in his pocket; he consulted it on all sorts of topics and regarded it as the infallible voice of God'. The Moravians give little attention to systematic theology... The Society's gatherings were characterized by an extraordinary fervour, but because of the lack of clear doctrinal teaching, its members proved susceptible to varying religious influences.[5]

On the positive side Pietism rejected cold orthodoxy and called believers back to the Scriptures, not just for intellectual knowledge but also for heart-felt change and authentic personal experience. On the negative side Pietism led to subjectivism which ultimately drew Christians away from truth as found in God's Word. Many church historians, including Mark Noll, believe that Pietism paved the way for the theological liberalism of the nineteenth and twentieth centuries. Others, but not all, see a link between unchecked Pietism and the Enlightenment. These are odd outcomes for a movement that attempted to bring the church back to the Scriptures and the proper application of truth. But they are not surprising outcomes given the dominate role that subjectivity ultimately played in the Pietistic movement. Once our lives and churches become untethered from the Scriptures there is no limit where they might land.

Where Did Pietism Go Wrong?

Of course that is a loaded question and presupposes that Pietism did go wrong. Given the fact that Pietism, to some degree, lives on in church-related groups as diverse as Amish, Methodist, Baptist, Pentecostal and the Amana Society it is hard to be precise. But, wherever experience and subjectivity reigns supreme over Scripture in the lives and churches of twenty-first-century believers there is something wrong. William Nix summarizes our concern well:

> Although Pietists adhered to the inspiration of the Bible, they advocated individual feeling as being of primary importance. That may have been an adequate method for avoiding cold orthodoxy of 'Protestant scholasticism', it opened the door for the equally dangerous enemy of 'subjective experientialism'. The first generation of Pietists could recall and reflect on its grounding in Scripture while validly advocating the need for individual experience. A second generation would stress the need for individual experience, but often without a proper Biblical or catechetical basis. This would leave a third generation that would question individual experience with no Biblical or doctrinal 'standard' to serve as an objective criterion. In turn, their unanswered questions would tend to demand an authority. When Scriptures were neglected, human reason or subjective experience would fill the need as the required 'standard'. Thus while not causing other movements Pietism gave impetus to three other movements in the post-Reformation church: deism, skepticism and rationalism.[6]

What Are the Implications for Today?

The great-grandchildren of Pietism live on in modern evangelicalism. On the positive side, much like the original Pietists there is a great hunger today for spirituality. People want a spirituality that works in the trenches of life. They want a faith that is relevant, provides answers and draws them closer to God. There is little interest in 'dead orthodoxy'. People want to feel something — experience something.

George Gallup documents this spiritual hunger in his book, *The Next American Spirituality*. Unfortunately much of the spirituality that he observes is without biblical foundation leading him to warn, 'Contemporary spirituality can resemble a grab bag of random experiences that does little more than promise to make our eyes mist up or our heart warm. We need perspective to separate the junk food from the wholesome, the faddish from the truly transforming.'[7] But perspective is hard to come by due to the massive level of biblical illiteracy, not only in America but among Christians as well. 'Half', Gallup says, 'of those describing themselves as Christians are unable to name who delivered the Sermon on the Mount. Many Americans cannot name the reason for celebrating Easter or what the Ten Commandments are. People think the name of Noah's wife was Joan, as in Joan of Ark.'[8] A high official in the Church of Scotland related a story in which his wife (a school teacher) had met a little boy in class who didn't even know what a Bible was.[9] I receive email from Australia, South Africa, The Netherlands and around the world lamenting the same thing — biblical illiteracy even among Christians.

Then there is what some have called 'the great disconnect' That is, there is a wide chasm between what people in the Western world in general, and self-proclaimed Christians in particular, claim to believe and how they live. While the general populace claim to have a great interest in spirituality, and Christians claim to be followers of Christ, our societies, homes and churches are inundated with corruption, violence, substance abuse, racism, divorce and materialism. This 'cluster of moral and theological shortcomings seemingly throws into question the transforming power of religious beliefs',[10] Gallup admits, leading him to state, 'Just because Americans claim they are more spiritual does not make them so.'[11] This leans into an excellent question, 'Is the church really rediscovering its spiritual moorings – or just engaging in retreat from seemingly insoluble problems?'[12]

Well, as baseball legend Yogi Berra once said, 'Prediction is very hard, especially when it's about the future', but if the New Testament is any indication, things don't look all that bright. The negative effect of Pietism, in many circles, is the development of Christians desiring a heart-felt faith who, nevertheless, have become increasingly distanced from the Word. Such spirituality may, as Gallup said, give us misty eyes and warm hearts but it does not create Christians who know Christ in terms described by the Bible. Paul clearly taught in Ephesians 4:11-16 that if we are to grow to maturity, equipped for the 'work of service' it will be as a result of biblical teaching from gifted leaders given to the church for that purpose. Without adequate biblical teaching we will be like children 'tossed here and there by waves, and carried about by every wind of doctrine' (v. 14). The perfect spiritual victims for deceitful schemers are those with warm hearts and empty heads. The church is full of folks today who have 'a zeal for God, but not in accordance with knowledge' (Rom. 10:2). They have a form of godliness but it is not biblically grounded. They are seeking feelings and experiences but not doctrinal truth. They are content to attend churches that do not expound the Scriptures, just as long as they are emotionally moved by the music or drama and comforted by relevant programs.

Such 'piety' is changing every facet of Christian and church life. Take worship for example. Monte E. Wilson has noted, 'For the modern evangelical, worship is defined exclusively in terms of the individual's experience. Worship, then, is not about adoring God but about being nourished with religious feelings, so much so that the worshiper has become the object of worship.'[13] The cause for this type of worship, Wilson believes, is the loss of devotion to Scriptures. He writes in pejorative terms, 'Others — probably the majority in modern American evangelicalism — have utterly neglected any commitment to the content of the Word and have ended with narcissistic "worship" services where everyone drowns in a sea of subjectivism and calls it "being bathed in the presence of the Holy Spirit." These people come to church exclusively to "feel" God.'[14] Some churches have even decided to call their worship services 'experiences'.[15]

Pietistic leanings, of course, are not limited to worship and the gathered church. Where they are most evident, and most concerning, is in the area of 'God's leading'. How does God speak to and lead his people according to Scripture? And how has Pietistic understanding of these things affected the way we interpret both Scripture and our subjective feelings? This will be the discussion in the pages that follow.

CHAPTER 2

THE LORD TOLD ME – I THINK!

In a newsletter published by a conservative Baptist denomination, a story is presented concerning one of its members. Deployed in Iraq, this middle aged soldier revealed that often, as he wrestles with problems of various types, 'God just reveals the answer to me.' A leader from his church back home also claims to have heard from the Lord. 'The Lord told me', he says, 'that this young man is going to be known as a builder, not a destroyer in Iraq.' So far his prophecy seems to have come true for, although the soldier has been involved in combat, his 'day job' is to rebuild schools and water treatment plants.

Recently I received an e-mail from a gentleman who wrote, 'Jesus has commanded me through the Holy Spirit to teach people how to pray, teach them the truth about their dreams, and guide them into the presence of God (utilizing the Scripture in an almost step-by-step methodology to do so).'

It seems the Lord has been quite busy lately speaking to his children. A few years ago Alistair Begg quoted a survey stating that one in three American adults say that God speaks to him directly.[1] And hearing the voice of God is not isolated to the common person either. A slew of evangelical leaders claim to hear from the Lord, some of them quite regularly. Henry Blackaby, an avid proponent of extra-biblical revelation of this type, when asked how he knew he was hearing from God and not from some other source, gives this answer, 'You come to know His voice as you experience Him in a love relationship. As God speaks and you respond, you will come to the point that you recognize His voice more and more clearly.'[2]

Is God Speaking Today?

Of course, that leaves dangling the important question, 'How does one know he is hearing the voice of the Lord in the first place?' Is it not possible that the voice many believe they are 'hearing' is the voice of their own thoughts, imaginations, desires, or something more insidious?

In vogue in much of evangelicalism is the constant imploring of Christians to listen to God, experience God and feel God. D. A. Carson quoting a friend's insightful critique of a book entitled *Listening to God*, wrote, 'If anyone had written a book thirty years ago with that title, you would have expected it to be about Bible study, not about prayer... Many [Christians] now rely far more on inward promptings than on their Bible knowledge to decide what they are going to do in a situation.'[3] There seems to have been a powerful shift in thinking among conservative Christians during the last few decades.

What does the New Testament Teach?

The final court of appeals determining the identity of the voice of God, if it is such, must be the direct instructions or at least the examples found in Scripture. The Scriptures claim to be the Word of God (2 Tim. 3:16, 17; 2 Peter 1:20, 21). They are inspired, once for all, by the Holy Spirit, enabling prophets and apostles, using their own personalities, to write God's words as he intended (Heb.1:1,2; 2:3,4; Acts 5:12; 2 Cor. 12:12). I believe **with the closure of Scripture, direct, infallible, authoritative revelation from God has ceased for this age** (Rev. 22:18, 19; Eph. 2:20; 3:5; Jude 3, 4; 2 Peter 3:2). It is instructive to note when Paul wrote his last epistle to pastor/friend Timothy about leading the church of God, he did not encourage Timothy to focus on new revelations, impressions, feelings or hunches. Rather, he **continually turned him to the Word of God and the doctrines contained therein** (2 Tim. 2:2-14, 15; 3:15-17; 4:2-4).

I find this to be the emphasis of the New Testament. As Donald S. Whitney reminds us,

> The evangelistic method of Jesus and the apostles was not to urge people to seek direct experiences with God; instead they went about preaching and teaching the Scriptures (see, for instance, Mark 1:14-15). And Jesus did not say that once we have spiritual life we live by direct mystical experience with God; rather, we 'live ... on every word that comes from the mouth of God' (Matthew 4:4). 'All Scripture is God-breathed and is useful for teaching, rebuking, correcting and training in righteousness, so that the man of God may be thoroughly equipped for every good work' (2 Timothy 3:16-17). That includes the 'good work' of growing in the knowledge of God and likeness to Christ. So in Scripture the normative method of meeting God is through Scripture.[4]

Other Issues to Consider

Yet, this type of divine encounter is considered insipid by many believers today. Many insist if God desires to relate to us in deep, personal, intimate ways, surely he must speak to us directly, individually, apart from Scripture. If we do not have such experiences, then we are nothing more than 'practical deists'. What has led to this mindset that teaches the Scriptures are inadequate for our lives — that some additional revelation is needed? Let me list three competitors now challenging the Scriptures as final authority in our lives.

Subjective Experience

In relation to our subject we must thoroughly wrestle with the question of how we know who or what we have encountered in our subjective experiences. All the information we have about God and our relationship to him is found in the Bible. Any 'encounter' apart from Scripture must be verified by Scripture. If

that is so, what does the Word tell us to expect in an encounter
with God? I think we will search in vain for information on what
God 'feels' like; instead the biblical record speaks of transformation. When we encounter God at the moment of salvation we
are born again (John 3). As Christians encounter God, through
the indwelling presence of the Holy Spirit, the mark is changed
lives (2 Peter 1).

D. Martin Lloyd-Jones was on to something when he
wrote,

> Let us imagine I follow the mystic way. I begin to have experiences; I
> think God is speaking to me; how do I know it is God who is speaking
> to me? How can I know I am not speaking to man; how can I be sure
> that I am not the victim of hallucinations, since this has happened
> to many of the mystics? If I believe in mysticism as such without the
> Bible, how do I know I am not being deluded by Satan as an angel
> of light in order to keep me from the true and living God? I have no
> standard... The evangelical doctrine tells me not to look into myself
> but to look into the Word of God; not to examine myself, but to look
> at the revelation that has been given to me. It tells me that God can
> only be known in His own way, the way which has been revealed in
> the Scriptures themselves.[5]

Of course, the current bent towards the subjective rather
than the biblical is nothing new. In each age it seems there are
pockets of God's people (sometimes bigger pockets than others)
who want to go beyond Scripture for their spiritual experiences.
Sinclair Ferguson writes,

> In Calvin's day, 'The Spiritual Ones' were a major thorn in the flesh
> to biblical reformation. Calvin despaired of helping people who felt
> the need to mention the Spirit in every second sentence they spoke!
> For the Puritans, the 'Inner Light' movement constituted a similar
> danger. In both cases 'what the Spirit said' and 'what the [human]
> spirit heard' were divorced from and then exalted over the Word. Put
> more brutally, subjective feeling and emotion reigned supreme over
> the objective revelation of Scripture. Similarly, today the subjective,

experiential, self-oriented, 'touchy-feely' secular mind of the 1960s has come home to roost in the evangelical world.[6]

'Our age', Udo W. Middelmann laments, 'has largely replaced real discussions of theological, philosophical, and cultural content with "personal" testimony, anecdotal experience, and private views.'[7]

A New Kind of Revelation — New Testament Prophecy

In Colossians 2:18, 19 Paul addresses a people confused by mystical experiences. The forerunners to the Gnostics taught that a few elite had received the gift of direct inspiration through the Holy Spirit. These moments of inspiration took place through visions, dreams and encounters with angels.[8] This divided the church into two classes, the haves and the have-nots (those who imagined themselves as truly spiritual and those who had not had these experiences).

This kind of problem has not faded into the past and is almost identical to the teachings found within various elements of the charismatic movement today. For example, compare what Jack Deere, a leading Vineyard theologian, writes:

> God can and does give personal words of direction to believers today that cannot be found in the Bible. I do not believe that he gives direction that contradicts the Bible, but direction that cannot be found in the Bible.[9]

But how does a person know if he is really hearing from God? Wayne Grudem, a highly regarded theologian who nevertheless is a wholesale believer in extra-biblical revelations of many kinds, answers:

> Did the revelation *seem like* something from the Holy Spirit; did it *seem* to be similar to other experiences of the Holy Spirit which he had known previously in worship. Beyond this it is difficult to specify much further, except to say that over time a congregation would *prob-*

ably become more adept at making evaluations ... and become more adept at recognizing a genuine revelation from the Holy Spirit and distinguishing it from their own thoughts (emphasis mine).[10]

Grudem is arguably one of the most careful and well-respected charismatic theologians in the world. He taught Biblical and Systematic Theology at Trinity International University in Deerfield, Illinois, for twenty years (which is affiliated with the Evangelical Free Churches of America). Yet, the best that he can devise in answer to our concern is, 'Did it **seem like** the Holy Spirit' and, 'A congregation would **probably**' be able to get better at discernment over time. While we are fumbling around trying to decide if something felt like the Holy Spirit (nothing in the Bible helps us here) and hoping that we will get better at discerning the voice of God, others, such as Henry Blackaby tell us that we dare not even make a move until we are certain that we have heard from God. Pity the poor Christian caught up in this confusion — he is hopelessly tossed about on a sea of subjectivity and mysticism.

At this point, Blackaby, Deere and Grudem would cry foul. They would claim that while they believe that God speaks to his people apart from the Bible today, these revelations are not on par with Scripture. That is, God speaks today but not with the same authority as he did in his Word. So do not accuse us of adding to Scripture, they would say. Interestingly enough, this brings up another issue. Does God ever speak in a non-authoritative manner? In the biblical record we find that God did speak, either orally (including through his prophets) or through the written Word. But always, **his Word was authoritative**. It was nothing less than a word from God — one that could be understood and must be obeyed and heeded! But we are being told today that God is speaking in a different, less authoritative way.

This is how Wayne Grudem explains it:

There is almost uniform testimony from all sections of the charismatic movement that prophecy is imperfect and impure, and will contain some elements which are not to be obeyed or trusted. The Anglican charismatic leaders Dennis and Rita Bennett write, 'We are not expected to accept every word spoken through the gifts of utterance ... but we are only to accept what is quickened to us by the Holy Spirit and is in agreement with the Bible ... one manifestation may be 75% God, but 25% the person's own thought. We must discern between the two.'[11]

But how? Where is Grudem taking us? Grudem's contention is that New Testament prophecy is different from Old Testament prophecy. True Old Testament prophecy was a direct revelation from God and thus infallible, with the prophet forfeiting his life if he was in error (Deut. 13:5; 18:20-22). But New Testament prophecy, including modern day efforts, so says Grudem, can be fallible. A New Testament prophecy could be partially from God and partially from ourselves. Thus, the Christian must attempt to discern where God leaves off and where man begins. And we are to make this determination without any insight from the New Testament which is totally silent on the subject. I believe Grudem to be in serious error, leaving the believer with no 'sure word of prophecy'. Nevertheless, his view is gaining popularity even among conservative theologians and leaders.

A New Kind of Revelation — the 'Inner' Voice

Non-charismatic evangelical Christianity has definitely taken on a mystical bent in recent days as well. While never denying the authority of Scripture as such, many, from people in the pew to key leaders, regularly point to mystical experiences as the basis for much of what they do and believe. We must be concerned that this weak view of the Scriptures will ultimately cause great harm in the body of Christ. We agree with David Wells' assessment, 'Granting the status of revelation to anything other than the Word of God inevitably has the effect of removing that status from the Word of God. What may start out as an additional authority alongside the Word of God will eventually supplant its authority altogether.'[12] John Armstrong concurs, 'Direct communication from God, by definition, constitutes some form of new revelation. Such revelation would, at least in principle, indicate that the Scriptures were not sufficient or final.'[13]

At issue is the subject of **revelation**. More to the point, is God speaking today, directly, infallibly, and independently of the Scriptures? Does he reveal himself, his will, his truth, apart from the Bible? Critics of the position presented in this paper will tell us to look at the examples found in Scripture. God seemed to be speaking all the time to all sorts of people, apart from the written Word. This is a clear overstatement, although there is surely some truth to be found. Let's make some observations. First, God did speak apart from the written Word occasionally. When we read the Bible we sometimes forget that what we are reading in a matter of minutes may have covered vast periods of time originally. Abraham, for example, definitely heard the voice of God at times. God speaks to him in Genesis 15 and again in Genesis 17. But there was at least a 14 year gap between the two utterances from God and possibly 20 years or more (compare 16:16 with 17:1). It seems to us that God was talking to Abraham almost daily but the fact is that many years would go by with no communication from God at all — even to Abraham the friend of God and father of the Jewish race. This leads to the next observation: when God did speak it was almost always to prophets and key players in the biblical story, not to the common man or woman. There may have been a few exceptions to this, but if so, it was rare. Yet, many today act as if God speaks to everyone all the time, and they attempt to prop up this view through biblical accounts. But the Scriptures simply do not support this idea.

There is a third observation that I believe is often missed and is of great importance to this discussion. When God did speak in Scripture, whether directly or through his prophets, he did so with audible words. You will search in vain for some inner voice from God speaking to the heart of his people. Nor will you find God communicating through prompting or hunches. No one said, 'I feel the Lord leading me to do such and such.' No one said, 'I have the peace of God in this decision.' In other words, God's people today have created a means of divine communication not found in the Bible. God never spoke in this fashion in Scripture, but we now are to believe that this is the norm today. In an otherwise excellent chapter on this same subject, R. Fowler White, who takes a cessationist view (with the closure of the Scriptures, God is no longer giving revelation for this age) opens the door to this form of communication by writing, 'God guides and directs His people by His Spirit in the application of His written word through promptings, impressions, insights, and the like.'[14] Vineyard theologian Jack Deere, in one of his few on-target remarks, sees clearly the weakness in White's statement,

> First, he doesn't offer a single text of Scripture to support his assertion that God's practical leading is carefully distinguished from the Spirit's work of revelation...White is simply asserting a distinction that not only can not be supported by Scripture, but, in fact, contradicts the Bible... [Secondly] how does White know God guides through promptings, impressions, insights, and the like? He can't use the Bible to prove this assertion... White is asking us to believe in a form of guidance that can't even be found in the Bible![15]

Fowler White has sent me personal correspondence stating that Deere has misunderstood the context of his comments, and that his position is not as Deere represents. I am unfortunately unclear as to exactly what White's views are in this regard. However, the position that Deere is identifying is held by many, and in this regard Deere is right. Many are telling us that God is speaking in a third way today, a way never found, described or hinted at in the Bible: God is speaking today but his Word is not authoritative, and what we think we are hearing can be weighed, examined and even dismissed. We are not even certain when and if he is speaking. And those who feel certain they are hearing from God still believe that the revelation may be impure and partly in error.

It remains a mystery to me why people are attracted to this view of revelation. *Surely* it is not an improvement over, 'Thus saith the Lord.' *Surely* the uncertainty of this system pales in comparison to the certainty of the Scriptures (2 Peter 1:19-21).

CHAPTER 3

GOD'S WILL, LOST OR FOUND?

A prestigious evangelical graduate school asked Professor X to accept a position as dean. In attempting to determine God's will on the matter, Professor X writes, 'While reading Acts 10 in Peterson's *The Message*, I read the words, "If God said it is okay, it is okay." I felt the Lord applying this Scripture to my situation; I knew then that I had permission to go.'

A well respected Christian author writes, 'When we feel the Master's hand and hear His voice in our *inner chambers*, we should follow Him' (emphasis mine). This same writer of devotional classics in one of his books heaped story upon story of the Lord leading through inner impressions and audible voices. He writes, 'It is positively exhilarating, and at the same time very humbling, to be in the company of men so intimately acquainted with God that they expect Him to even direct them in which house to visit, what tide to take, or what stranger to speak to on the trail.'

This concept of how the Lord leads is so commonplace today that the above examples probably shocked none of my readers. And this is not just a modern phenomenon — such views can be traced throughout church history. For example, take the Puritan pastor Cotton Mather (1663-1728), one of the most influential religious figures in early American history. While doctrinally sound in most ways, Mather had a strange belief in what he termed 'particular faiths'. He meant by the term, 'A little degree of the *Spirit of Prophecy* granted by God to the devotional elite for abounding in secret prayer' (emphasis his).[1] Mather believed that angels administered these 'particular faiths' which would guarantee answers to prayer and provide infallible divine leading. For many years he had absolute faith in 'divine leadings', until a large number of the messages supposedly from God proved to be false. This included the death of his wife and the spiritual condition of his son. Because of disillusionment with 'particular faiths', Mather's own faith almost unravelled. He speculated for a time that the problem may actually lie with the angels (whom he believed transmitted these messages from God). Perhaps, he mused, they may actually be ignorant of the future themselves. Of course, this did not solve the problem. If God was leading him through angels and yet that leading was fallible, of what good was the leading? Finally, he came to realize that he had misinterpreted these impressions, became cautious and abandoned them as if of no value.[2]

We are faced with the same dilemma. Does God lead his children through extra-biblical means or not? To what extent would such leading be reliable? Could extra-biblical leadings (if they existed) be trusted completely, partially or not at all? How would we know? Our only hope for a comprehensive answer, as always, is not in the testimonies and experiences of people but in examination of the sufficient Word of God.

The Will of God for My Life

We constantly overhear in Christian circles that someone is looking for the will of God for his life. He is most likely speaking of the major decisions — who to marry, where to attend school, what vocation to follow, etc. Others are seeking God's will for slightly lesser concerns: what car or house to buy, church to attend, vacation to take. We have been taught that the will of God can be ascertained through divinely prompted feelings, hunches, impressions or dreams. If these fail we can turn to fleeces, fasting, flipping coins or opening the Bible randomly and following the first verse that makes sense. To be sure, these methods are usually coupled with analysis of circumstances, wise counsel, and the peace of God. But here a serious question arises — does the Bible prescribe such methods? Is this how God says we are to discern his will?

The first step in answering these questions is to discover what the Scriptures have to say about God's will. Most Christians use the term 'the will of God' in three distinct ways. First, there is the sovereign will of God in which it is recognized that our Lord is in control of all things in the universe. Ephesians 1:11 reads, '… having been predestined according to His purpose who works all things after the counsel of His will.' While certain aspects of God's sovereign will are revealed to us in Scripture, other parts are not for us to know at this time (Deut. 29:29). Nevertheless, the Word is clear that God rules over all things and his plans can never be thwarted. Resting in this truth brings lasting peace to the hearts of God's children regardless of circumstances.

Secondly, Scripture speaks of the revealed will of God which makes known to us how God expects us to live. Paul writes, 'Finally then, brethren, we request and exhort you in the Lord Jesus, that, as you received from us instruction as to how you ought to walk and please God (just as you actually do walk), that you may excel still more. For you know what commandments we gave you by the authority of the Lord Jesus. For this is the will of God, your sanctification, that is, that you abstain from sexual immorality' (1 Thess. 4:1-3). This is just one example of the revealed will of God for lives. It is God's revealed will that we be sanctified or, in this context, live in purity. It is also his revealed will that we love him and that we love our neighbour. It is God's revealed will that we worship and obey him, and so forth. The Bible clearly teaches both the sovereign and revealed will of God.

It is the third understanding of the will of God, the specific or individual, which demands our attention. While not a position held by Garry Friesen he nevertheless defines it well, 'God's ideal, detailed life-plan uniquely designed for each believer.'[3] He further frames the issue by writing, 'This life-plan encompasses every decision we make and is the basis of God's daily guidance. This guidance is given through the indwelling Holy

Spirit who progressively reveals God's life-plan to the heart of the individual believer. The Spirit uses many means to reveal this life-plan... but He always gives confirmation at the point of each decision.'[4] Most espousing this view are content to suppose that God reveals his will only for major decisions, but others take this to the extreme of believing that God has a will which we must find for even the most minute thing, from which shoes to wear to what route to take to work.

The question on the table is whether the 'individual-will-of-God' theory can be supported by Scripture. That God is at work behind the scenes, leading and directing our lives, is not the question, in this all conservative Christians agree. The question is whether the Bible teaches that God has specific will(s) for each of us — specific choices he wants us to make on all sorts of things — and whether these will(s) must be discerned through various extra-biblical means. I believe, contrary to the majority of Christians, that the answer to these questions is a clear 'no'.

The Biblical Evidence

I believe the support for my position can be found first from the silence of Scripture. The Bible nowhere teaches that God has a specific will for every believer's life that is to be found through extra-biblical means. Yes, we have numerous examples in the Word in which God specifically directed his people to take a course of action. But I would raise a number of objections at this point:

- The fact that a few individuals received direct guidance from God does not mean that such guidance was then, or is now, normative. If certain things happened in the Holy Writ does that mean they will happen all the time or that they will necessarily happen to us? Balaam's donkey spoke to him but I don't expect my dog to speak to me. Peter walked on water for a while but I wouldn't try it. Elijah called fire out of heaven, but I can't even light my gas grill half the time. Even if it can be proven that it was customary for God to reveal his specific will to people in biblical times, it does not necessarily prove that such is God's plan today. Proof by example is weak evidence at best.

•   Secondly, these examples are far fewer than most people think. Yes, God spoke and directed Moses on a regular basis, David and Peter on occasion, Solomon two or three times and a host of others in a singular instance. But there is no evidence, in either Testament, that the vast number of believers ever received such guidance. With rare exception, only the major players in biblical history enjoyed the direct supervision of God — the masses, even of the godly, lived their entire lives without a personal word from the Lord.

•   Even guidance given to the key characters of Scripture was rare and reserved for a handful of decisions. God spoke most often in biblical times through the prophets, yet even major prophets could go years without a word from God. Many others who walked powerfully with God and accomplished much for his glory never once heard from God, to our knowledge. I think of Nehemiah, Ezra, Esther, Ruth, David's mighty men and thousands of others — the list is almost endless. As a matter of fact, the vast majority of the godly found in Scripture never personally heard from God concerning their individual lives and decisions. The ones of which we are aware were the exceptions, not the rule.

•   Even the exceptions received guidance only for the most important matters — almost exclusively matters pertaining to the big scheme of God's plan. Except as object lessons and/or messages intended for a wider audience, we hear of no instances in which a biblical character was told specifically what choices to make concerning normal matters of life such as household purchases, investments, even who to marry except for the case of Isaac — and even that was indirect and Hosea as an object lesson to Israel. It was just not the norm in the Bible for God's people to be given specific instruction on a regular basis from the Lord. Most never received such instruction even once — and apparently never expected it.

✷ • While God chose to occasionally give special leading to a few of the important New Testament leaders, we never find those individuals seeking such guidance (or being commanded to do so). Peter was sleeping on a roof, Paul was headed to a different country, Philip was involved in a preaching campaign. All of them were busy serving the Lord when he chose to redirect them. As a matter of fact, the last time we find an example of God's people seeking his specific will is in Acts 1:24-26 with the choosing of Matthias to be an apostle. And here they do not hear the voice of God, or even feel a prompting but rely on a game of chance. It is altogether questionable to me that the right decision was made through this methodology. Later Christ would handpick Paul as Judas' replacement, leaving little room for Matthias to be one of the Twelve.[5]

God's Leading

Assuming for the moment that God, in this New Testament era, has changed plans and has made extra-biblical leading by means of the Holy Spirit the norm, exactly how should we expect this to take place? Most evangelicals outside of charismatic circles do not expect God to communicate with them through prophets, audible voices, visions, the casting of lots, angelic visitations or the Urim and Thummim (Exod. 28:30), yet these were the instruments used in biblical times when God chose to lead apart from the written Word. Today the majority of evangelicals believe that God leads through other means, usually highly subjective ones such as hunches, promptings, open doors or peace (or lack thereof). In Scripture, however, when God chose to communicate, the transmission was objective. While there were times when the interpretation of these messages was complex, there was never any doubt that God had spoken (through some understandable vehicle). We don't hear of Isaiah, for instance, saying, 'God spoke to me last night, I think, and I believe he wants you Israelites to do such-and-such, but then again, I am not absolutely sure of this. After all, it is often difficult to tell when the voice of God leaves off and my own thoughts take over. And, of course, there is always that pesky problem of interpretation. I know what I heard, but I may possibly confuse the message. My prophecy may then be 50% from God and 50% from my own imagination, but I will lay it out before you and let you discern whether and how much the Holy Spirit has actually said through me.'

We never hear of God speaking in this manner in the Bible but we are being told that it is common place today, especially in charismatic and mystical circles. Unfortunately the problem becomes even more complex in non-charismatic settings, since non-charismatics are often expecting God to lead and speak to them in ways never mentioned in Scripture. We will search in vain for instances in which God led his people through hunches and promptings. And, equally, we will search in vain for occurrences of New Testament believers asking God for his individual will or, for that matter, explaining their decisions as springing from God's individual will communicated to them through feelings.

Take the example of the folks in James 4:13-17 who arrogantly announce their business plans without regard to the will of God.

> Come now, you who say, 'Today or tomorrow we will go to such and such a city, and spend a year there and engage in business and make a profit.' Yet you do not know what your life will be like tomorrow. You are just a vapor that appears for a little while and then vanishes away. Instead, you ought to say, 'If the Lord wills, we will live and also do this or that.' But as it is, you boast in your arrogance; all such boasting is evil. Therefore, to one who knows the right thing to do and does not do it, to him it is sin.

James does not admonish these believers for neglecting to first seek the specific will of God in the matter; he simply is saying that our plans must always be subject to the sovereign will of God. The Lord is at liberty to adjust or cancel any of our plans and the believer must live in recognition of this fact. The implication is that, since none of us can know God's will in advance, we must humbly accept his sovereign will when it becomes evident. This is the pattern found throughout the New Testament.

In 1 Corinthians 7, the apostle Paul is dealing with one of the most important decisions in life — marriage. What a perfect opportunity to lay out the steps for discernment of the specific will of God. Instead the Holy Spirit-inspired apostle, after some advice pertinent to the current situation, leaves the decision as to whether one should marry to the individual believer (vv. 8-9, 20-21). Then to top things off, he even leaves the decision as to whom she is to marry to the individual, as long as she marries another believer (v. 39). Why didn't the apostle take this golden opportunity to lay out the principles for finding the individual will of God? I mean, outside of our relationship with the Lord, what could be more important than whom (if anyone) we should marry? Yet we find this decision being left up to the believer within biblical parameters.

Seeking the individual will of the Lord is so out of alignment with New Testament teaching that Professor Bruce K. Waltke wrote a book suggesting that it was basically a pagan notion rather than a biblical one.[6] He writes,

> When we seek to 'find' God's will, we are attempting to discover hidden knowledge by supernatural activity. If we are going to find His will on one specific choice, we will have to penetrate the divine mind to get His decision. 'Finding' in this sense is really a form of divination. The idea was common in pagan religions. As a matter of fact, it was the preoccupation of pagan kings... But that sort of pagan behavior is what Christ saved us out of.[7]

Is Waltke correct or has he overstated his case? That can be determined only by the examination of Scripture.

Chapter 4

Impressions and Scriptures

In Dave Swavely's helpful book, *Decisions, Decisions,* he writes:

> Many Christians, who would say that they do not believe in new revelation, are essentially seeking new revelation in their decision making. They may have a theology of 'cessationism' in their view of revelation, but in their everyday practice they contradict that theology by trying to hear God say something that is not in the Bible. And I would suggest that their theology is right, so they should let it shape their practical living. God is speaking today, but he is speaking through his Word.[1]

But can't we have it both ways? Can't we have the completed revelation of God in the Bible and extra-biblical revelations, which do not quite approach inspiration, on the side? O. Palmer Robinson suggests that we can't:

> And why not both? Why not the illumination of Scripture coupled with new revelations of the Spirit? Simply because if you declare a need for both, you have implied the insufficiency of the one. You have placed yourself back in the framework of the old covenant, in a time when the new revelations were required because of the incompleteness of the old. But Christ is the final word.[2]

On the other side of the fence are those who say that such theology is practical deism, robbing us of a personal God who is at work in us individually. Scripture, they would say, is unquestionably the inspired Word of God — but it is God's Word for everyone equally. When I read that the 'Lord is my Shepherd' or that Christ died for our sins, these are true statements, but they are true for every believer not just for me. How would you like it, they ask, if your wife said she loved you but she loved you equally to everyone she knows? Would that make you feel special or just one of many? So it is with God and us. He claims to love the world and he has spoken in general to all (through the Bible), but we also need personal words — words just to us, to affirm our personal relationship. And part of that personal word includes guidance. If the Lord really loves me and he is all-wise, then I need his intimate instructions. It is not enough, once again, that he has given broad instructions, principles and guidance to everyone. I need something more, something just for me, something private. The Scriptures tell me that God leads me in the paths of righteousness — and that is good. But I need his leading in more specific issues such as job selection, which person to marry, what house to buy and dozens of other concerns. I don't need his help in choosing what clothes to wear or which route I should take to church (apparently there is a threshold below which I am capable of making my own choices), but for life's big decisions I need a personal message.

What these folks are saying seems to make sense but are they correct? It would appear that a number of passages of Scripture indicated that they are not. What if, as Garry Friesen says, impressions are not authoritative but are really just impressions?[3] What if they are not communications from God at all, I mean, unbelievers have impressions, don't they? What is the source of their impressions? Let's see what the Bible says.

But What about Those Scriptures?

Psalm 19 teaches us there are two sources of revelation, nature (vv. 1-6) and Scripture (vv. 7-14). The 'general revelation' of nature, while speaking boldly of the glory of God, nevertheless has

serious limitations. Romans 1:20 confirms that nature is capable
of revealing to mankind the eternal power and divine nature of
God; therefore even those who know nothing of Jesus Christ
are without excuse when they reject God. But general revelation
is incapable of exposing a multitude of things including Jesus
Christ, the Cross, grace, eternal life and on and on. For such
things we need the 'specific revelation' of Scripture. These two,
general and specific revelations, have been recognized by God's
people throughout the ages as the normal ways in which God
communicates to us. Occasionally, the Lord breaks through in
other ways, whether by angels, visions, dreams and even donkeys, but these are rare exceptions as we have explored previ-
ously.

But to these have been added another form of communication, one not found in the Word — that of the inner voice of God
in one way or another. While we have already found that this inner voice is absent in Scripture (the 'still small voice' that Elijah
heard in 1 Kings 19:12-13 is often presented as evidence of the
inner voice of God, but even a quick look at the passage shows
that this was a literal 'outer' voice, not an inner impression), still
there are a number of texts that would appear to indicate that
God leads in this New Testament era apart from Scripture. That
is, to be clear, God seems in these passages to be communicating specific instructions about our individual lives through extra-
biblical sources, most often through circumstances, impressions
and godly counsel. That in decision making the Christian would
be wise to pay careful attention to these matters is not up for
debate. The question is whether God is actually communicating
his particular will for a particular individual through these particular means. I believe the answer is a clear 'no'.

But what about the Scriptures which seem to imply that
God does have a specific will and he will lead us in it if we meet
certain conditions? These Scriptures include: Proverbs 3:5, 6;
Colossians 1:9-10; 3:15; Philippians 4:6, 7; Romans 8:14, 16;
Psalm 32:8; John 16:12-14 and Ephesians 5:17. Let's take a
quick look at some of the more pertinent passages to see what
they are actually teaching in context.

Romans 8:14 — 'For all who are being led by the Spirit of God, these are the sons of God.' A common interpretation of this verse is that one of the ways we know we are actually sons of God is through the inner leading of the Holy Spirit in our lives. If we are born again we should expect the Holy Spirit to confirm our spiritual condition by the steady reception of extra-biblical, supernatural direction from the Holy Spirit about personal decisions. But the context of the passage has nothing to do with decision making and everything to do with holy living. The evidence of our conversion, Paul is saying, is the leading of the Holy Spirit in our lives — but that leading is towards righteous living not decision making (vv. 9-13). I agree with Don Matzat on this verse,

> Bible teachers generally agree that when the apostle Paul tells us to be led by the Spirit, he is not speaking of some momentary external invasion of the Holy Spirit into our consciousness, telling us what to do and how to do it. Nor is he referring to our effort to conjure up the Spirit in some mystical encounter. Paul is simply telling us to live according to our new life in Christ, which is Christ dwelling in us by His Holy Spirit, or to be 'led by the Spirit' as opposed to living according to our old sinful nature, or being 'led by the flesh'.[4]

Romans 8:16 — 'The Spirit Himself testifies with our spirit that we are children of God.' Doesn't this verse speak of an inner witness of the Holy Spirit? Even if we recognize that the context concerns evidence of spiritual life and not decision making, isn't Paul saying that a Christian will know he is saved because the Holy Spirit is somehow speaking to his heart?

Well first, even if that were true, we are not told how the Holy Spirit 'testifies with our spirit'. Many run to the conclusion that this witness is an inner voice or impression by which we feel the presence of God through the Holy Spirit and thus know we are saved. But I do not believe that interpretation can be confirmed from this verse. To start, the verse does not say that the Holy Spirit witnesses to our spirit but 'with' our spirit. In other words, when the Holy Spirit and our spirit are in agreement, we know we are saved. When the witness of the believer's spirit, as to why he believes he is a child of God, agrees with the witness of the Holy Spirit (the Spirit-inspired gospel as recorded in the Bible), then he knows he is a child of God.

Psalm 37:4 — On the basis of this verse, 'Delight yourself in the Lord and He will give you the desires of your heart', some conclude that believers living in conformity with the Lord are able to trust their desires to lead them. Calvin is reported to have said, 'Love God and do as you please.' But this interpretation pushes the verse too far and runs counter to other Scriptures. The normal understanding of this verse is that, when we delight in the Lord, it will result in changing our desires so that they are in harmony with God's desires for us. But the Psalm does not go on to say our desires are now totally trustworthy. Our flesh is at war with the Spirit for as long as we are in these bodies (Gal. 5:16-18), making it difficult to always know that our heart's desires are pure. Paul seemed to struggle with conflicting desires on a regular basis (Rom. 7:14-25) and he desired to go to Spain but never did (Rom. 15:24, 28). Even Jesus desired to avoid the Cross but chose to submit himself to the will of the Father (Matt. 26:36-46). The desires of the committed Christian may be a good starting place in our decision making process, but we cannot biblically claim that our desires have been implanted by the Spirit, or that they are infallible guides.

Philippians 4:6-7 coupled with Colossians 3:15 are verses that have been used by multitudes of believers who seek the 'peace of God' in their decision making.

> Be anxious for nothing, but in everything by prayer and supplication with thanksgiving let your requests be made known to God. And the peace of God, which surpasses all comprehension, will guard your hearts and your minds in Christ Jesus.

> Let the peace of Christ rule in your hearts, to which indeed you were called in one body and be thankful.

The argument goes like this: the final arbitrator (ruler) in knowing God's will is the peace of God. If the Lord wants us to take action he will indicate his approval by giving us his peace. On the other hand, if we are not in the will of God, the Lord will make this obvious through unrest in our hearts.

As a young man trying to apply the 'peace of God' theory to my life, I ran into some very practical problems. For example, I could never get God's peace when it came to major purchases. I 'desired' a new car (was this a desire from God or not?) but I was too much of a penny-pincher to have 'peace' about spending large chunks of money. I was at a stalemate. I had no peace about buying the car but no peace about not buying it either. Somehow the peace theory (or even the desire theory for that matter) wasn't working for me. I assumed I was either too sinful or too stupid to discern God's peace. Then I observed people claiming God's peace over the dumbest of decisions — decisions that would come back to haunt them. It wasn't until years later I was relieved to revisit these passages and discover that they were not in the context of decision making at all. Both passages were talking about peace (or lack of conflict) between the believer and other people and/or God, not some inner peace that would indicate when we have made the right choices. Harmony with our fellow man and God by living out his revealed will is the context, not decision making.

2 Corinthians 2:12-13 — And what about those open doors? This passage reads, 'Now when I came to Troas for the gospel of Christ and when a door was opened for me in the Lord, I had no rest for my spirit, not finding Titus my brother; but taking my leave of them, I went on to Macedonia.' Verses that speak of open doors (see also, Acts 14:27; 1 Cor.16:8, 9; Col. 4:3) 'open the door' for us to examine the role circumstances play in the specific will of God. Are circumstances God's way of communicating his will to us? Scripture does not indicate that they are.

One of the problems with circumstances is their subjective nature; that is, we can read into them just about anything we want. If we can't find a good job in our home town, is this God's way of telling us to move or his way of wringing materialism out of our souls? If we interpret that it is God's will for us to move, just where is He leading? Certainly the Lord was direct with Paul's call to Macedonia, but that was a unique move on the Lord's part involving a vision, not just a change in circumstances. Of course, if the Lord opens a door, or closes one (something never mentioned in the Bible), we need to take a good look. But even these open doors are not authoritative. Paul prayed for open doors for the gospel, asking for opportunity to spread the good news, yet in 2 Corinthians 2:12-13 God had given him an open door which he chose to ignore because he had other things on his mind. At best, circumstances represent opportunities (or lack thereof) which may help us in our decisions but are not mandates from God. If, for instance, I believe I have been 'called' to preach but no one seems to be called (or are willing) to listen, the examination of that circumstance may prove most helpful. But it neither confirms nor negates whether I ought to be a pastor, although it could supply helpful data in my vocational choices.

Proverbs 3:5-6 — 'Trust in the Lord with all your heart and do not lean on your own understanding, in all of your ways acknowledge Him, and He will make your paths straight.'

This is surely one of the most beloved passages in the Word and rightly so. During great moments of stress and doubt what believer has not read or quoted these words with great comfort? But just what is being promised to those who trust and acknowledge the Lord? The understanding of the passage is skewed by the KJV rendering of the final phrase, which reads, 'and he shall direct thy paths'. The implication, at least to many, is that the Lord will direct us in his perfect and specific will for our lives if we will but trust in him. The problem with this understanding of the passage is that the word 'path' does not reference a specific will in the Old Testament usage, but speaks of the general path of life. In Proverbs 4:18 we hear of the 'path of righteousness'. And in Proverbs 15:19 we are told that 'the path of the upright is a highway'. Proverbs 11:5 gives a similar promise as 3:6 when it says, 'The righteousness of the blameless will smooth his way.'

What we have then is not a promise of an individual direction found through trusting God, but a description of the type of life that the trusting lead. It is a life in compliance with the moral or revealed will of God. Those who lean on him are going the right direction in the path of life. They are living as God would have the righteous live. Friesen says it well, 'The point of Proverbs 3:5-6, then, is that those who trust God, and trust in His wisdom rather than their own worldly understanding, and acknowledge God in each part of their life, will reap a life that is successful by God's standards.'[5]

John 14:26 — 'But the Helper, the Holy Spirit, whom the Father will send in My name, He will teach you all things, and bring to your remembrance all that I said to you.'

John 16:12-14 — 'I have many more things to say to you, but you cannot bear them now. But when He, the Spirit of truth, comes, He will guide you into all the truth; for He will not speak on His own initiative, but whatever He hears, He will speak; and He will disclose to you what is to come. He shall glorify Me; for He shall take of Mine, and shall disclose it to you.'

Many take these verses to have universal application. But are we to read these passages as a promise for all believers at all times, or are these promises peculiar to the apostles and indicators of the New Testament revelation that would soon be given them through the Holy Spirit? John 14:12 especially has been used by many to support either continuing revelation or unique illumination, but such an interpretation is hobbled by the closing phrase which promises to 'bring to your remembrance all that I said to you'. Jesus was clearly speaking of instructions given to the apostles while he was walking among them. Much of what he taught them was beyond their comprehension. This discourse found in John 14-16 contained some of the deepest theology ever given by our Lord and was easily beyond the grasp of the apostles. He therefore promises them that in the future a Helper will come, the Holy Spirit, who will bring these things back to their remembrance and even guide them into

new revelation (16:13-14). I do not believe Jesus is referencing
individual decision making concerning the routine areas of life.
Rather he is speaking of the method by which the Lord would
transmit New Testament truth to the church (see 1 Cor. 2:9-
10).

A Personal Application

As I write this chapter I am sitting on a veranda in Brazil. Some
months ago I was invited by some Brazilian pastors to come to
their country and minister at a pastors' conference, preach in
several churches and present lectures on contemporary theological issues at a seminary. When invited, I had a decision to
make. The opportunities to present the Word, teach and encourage Brazilian church leadership and other believers were
enormous. But on the other hand the trip would be expensive
and I would have to be gone from my own church and family
for seventeen days. How was I to decide the 'Lord's will' in this
matter? A door of opportunity was open, but I would be forfeiting other opportunities. I could seek the Lord's peace but I was
on the horns of my usual dilemma — peace either way was
elusive. I sought the counsel of my church elders and they said,
'Do whatever you want' — big help they were. If only the Lord
would tell me what to do, or a least give me some strong impressions, then I might know what to do, but no promptings were
forthcoming. In the end I made a decision to come to Brazil, a
decision that I believe was one that honoured the Lord. But if
the Lord wasn't 'leading' me to come to Brazil, how do I know
whether I am in his will? Without impressions, promptings, the
Lord's peace, or definitive circumstances, how do I know that I
made the right decision? Or could I have stayed home and still
been in his will?

CHAPTER 5

FREEDOM TO CHOOSE

In our discussion of God's will, the issue is not whether God
has a specific, sovereign plan for our lives. Deuteronomy 29:29
tells us, 'The secret things belong to the Lord our God, but the
things revealed belong to us and to our sons forever, that we
may observe all the words of this law.' This verse adds a lot of
insight into how God wants us to live. The 'things revealed', the
Scriptures, have been given to us in order that we might live
according to God's revealed (sometimes called moral) will. But
what about the secret things — the things hidden, the things
not made known in the Word? Those things belong to God
— they are God's plan, concealed from us. The point is, rather
than attempting to penetrate the heavens to search out the hidden mysteries of God, we should concentrate on what God has
disclosed to us. It is the revealed things that enable us to live in
conformity to the ways of God.

But what about the hidden things? There are things not
found on the pages of Scripture, things we often want to know.
The Bible doesn't tell me whether I should be married and it
certainly does not tell me whom to marry. Don't we need additional information from God apart from Scripture? And if so,
don't we need some methodology, some technique, for discovering this information? In reply, we might explore a couple of
matters:

•   Has God instructed us to search for his specific will? I believe the answer is 'no'. There exist no teachings, commands or examples to, or for, Holy-Spirit-indwelt, New Testament Christians to seek God's individual will about anything. Not where to live or whom to marry, not even whether someone should be in 'full-time' Christian ministry. In the New Testament, we find believers busy serving and living for the Lord whatever their circumstances. We do not find them running about seeking a directive from God before they made decisions.

On the other hand, if God chose to redirect someone, he did so and there was never any ambivalence about what he was saying. For example, as Paul begins his second missionary journey, we do not find him and Barnabas seeking the Lord's will. Instead Paul said to Barnabas, 'Let us return and visit the brethren…' (Acts 15:36). In the midst of the journey, God chose to intervene and sent Paul to Macedonia (Acts 16:6-10). The important thing to note is that this change in plans was initiated by God. Paul was not seeking God's will in the matter; he was busy ministering. It was God who chose to intervene and, of course, Paul was immediately obedient.

✳ I believe this is the same type of thing that we encounter in James 4:13-17. James was not condemning these Christian businessmen for making plans for business or desiring to make a profit. He warned them of their presumptuous attitude which left God out of the equation. In verse fifteen James instructs, 'Instead, you ought to say, "If the Lord wills, we shall live and also do this or that."' What a perfect place for James to write, 'Before you make business plans you must first seek the Lord's will.' But he does not. He wants them only to be aware and open to the sovereign hand of God that may alter their adventure. I believe this is the biblical pattern for church age Christians.

•   If my thesis is correct, we should expect to find in the New Testament numerous examples and admonishments for believers to make decisions that are in accordance with the revealed will of God. And that is exactly what we find. To proof-text this fact would be to proof text the entire New Testament

Scriptures, but we will take the opportunity to turn our attention to some passages.

Freedom

Let's narrow our search to those decisions in life for which Christians commonly seek an extra-biblical word from the Lord.

Personal Preferences

Just as today, the early Christians had trouble accepting the concept that other Christians might see things differently. We are most comfortable when everyone agrees with us — after all, our preferences are hopefully based on principles drawn from Scripture. So what happens when others don't accept our logic and choose to reject our preferences? In a word, conflict. Paul writes Romans 14 to deal with this very scenario. The apostle's inspired counsel is neither to seek the peace of God nor to recommend a method to discern who is right, but to accept one another (v. 2) and let God be the judge (v. 4).

Let's frame this with a modern day example. First Church needs a new building — about this all are agreed, but there the unanimity ends. Brother Joe wants to move to Third Street, but Brother Bill believes God would have them move to the countryside. Sister Suzy, treasurer and professional financial planner, believes the church can easily handle a $500,000 mortgage, but Sister Jane has no peace about debt. How is all of this to be settled? Pastor Jim is praying for a word from the Lord to bring back to his people, but about the time he thinks God has spoken to him, head-deacon George claims a contradictory word from God. The fight is on.

Has the Lord left us to such subjective means to determine the best thing to do in such a situation? I think not. Romans 14 lays down timeless principles for handling differences of opinion. The passage is not going to tell First Church whether they should build, where, with or without debt, but it will tell the congregation how the body of Christ is to handle disagreement and varied preferences.

Giving

How much should we give to the Lord's work? Should we just tithe and be done with it? If so, do we tithe off the net or the gross (if you come from my background you know what I am talking about)? Does our tithe all go to our home church ('storehouse tithing' some call it) or can we spread it around? If we don't buy the tithing system, where do we turn? What pastor hasn't said, 'We want you to give as the Lord lays it on your heart?' Is this the biblical principle? Are we to expect the Lord to lay a certain amount on our hearts and, while he is at it, to tell us who to give it to as well?

To find answers to all of these questions we would do well to turn to 2 Corinthians 8-9, the most comprehensive section in Scripture on New Testament giving. There we find none of the above suggestions but a whole different set of directions. Many instructions and motivations are given but the bottom line is, 'Let each one do just as he has purposed in his heart' (9:7). No prayer is made for God to lay a burden on our hearts. No demand to tithe is given — just 'as he has purposed in his heart'. Of course God loves a cheerful giver (9:7), giving is a great privilege (8:2-6), giving is to be liberal (8:2), giving is to be motivated by Christ's indescribable gift (8:9; 9:15) and giving is to be proportionate to our financial blessedness (1 Cor. 16:2). Still we are giving as we purpose in our heart.

Marriage

Few decisions in life can compare to the decision we make concerning a spouse. If ever we could use a word from the Lord it would be in regard to whom to marry. I remember, during my freshman year at Bible college, when one of the seniors, a spiritual 'giant' in the student body, took an attractive young freshman out on a date and promptly informed her that God had told him that she would be his wife. She was in shock but this young man, after all, was a spiritual giant, well respected by students and faculty alike; who was she to stand in the way of the Lord? If it was the Lord's will then she must accept it. But presumably the Lord changed his mind somewhere down the line, for the spiritual giant married someone else, much to the relief, I might add, of the young freshman.

If the Lord has an ideal mate picked out for us how are we to know? If there is one area in which we don't want to miss God's perfect will this has to be it. Yet nowhere in the New Testament are we taught anything about finding God's handpicked 'one and only'. In 1 Corinthians 7, in which the Lord discusses numerous marriage-related problems and concerns, we are actually given different instructions. Paul writes in verse thirty-nine, 'A wife is bound as long as her husband lives; but if her husband is dead, she is free to be married **to whom she wishes**, only in the Lord' (emphasis mine). Again if there ever was a place to lay out the steps for finding the perfect mate it was right here. But Paul says that she is free to marry whomever she wishes, as long as he is a believer. That does not mean there are not other biblical criteria for choosing a mate, but the point is the choice is left to the believer. There is no mention in Scripture that God has the 'one' picked out for you and, that if you marry someone else you will miss out on God's perfect plan for your life.

In General

What is the normative pattern in the New Testament for decision making? Paul told Titus, 'I have decided to spend the winter [at Nicopolis]' (Titus 3:12), not 'the Lord has led me to do so'. Paul stayed in Athens by himself while sending Timothy to Thessalonica because 'we thought it best' (1 Thess. 3:1-2), not because the Lord had given him peace about it. When Paul sent Epaphroditus back to the Philippians he did so because he 'thought it necessary' (Phil. 2:25), not because the Lord had laid it on his heart. The Corinthians were to pick 'whomever you may approve' to accompany Paul with their financial gift for he saw it as 'fitting for me to go also' (1 Cor. 16:3-4). No mention is made about seeking the Lord's will in this.

Decision Making

When we come to the New Testament searching for how God would have us make decisions, what categories do we find? Rather than directions on how to discern the individual will of God we are given principles of decision making. Rather than pointing us to hunches, inner voices and promptings, we are pointed to scriptural guidelines that enable us to make wise choices to the glory of God. The New Testament paints a picture of a believer who knows and obeys Scripture, indwelt and empowered by the Holy Spirit, and who has been given a mind whereby he is able to think, reason, discern and choose. He is an individual who is quite capable (due to regeneration, the Scriptures and the renewing of his mind) of making wise decisions which please God.

It is for these reasons that God does not call for Christians to make subjective choices based upon what they 'feel' God might be telling them. Rather we are to be students of the Word, knowing how God wants us to reason and choose based upon principles he has given us. It would be far easier, and to some it would appear more spiritual, to have God tell us our every move. Why diligently search the Scriptures to discern the most prudent pathway when we can just close the Book, shut our eyes and listen to God's inner voice? Of course, if the New Testament informed us that this is how God leads us today, then we go with it. But you will search in vain for such teaching.

So, what does the New Testament say about decision making?

Always begin with Scripture. A plethora of problems, mistakes, errors and false living could be avoided if we would just begin with Scripture. This is a simple principle that is far too often ignored. The habit of many, even many Christian leaders, is to begin with an idea, philosophy, personal preference, pet peeve or observation, and then go back to Scripture to find a few verses to support their theory. If we do that, we might be able to convince ourselves of almost anything. But if all we do and believe emerges from the Word itself, we will be able to discern the value, or lack thereof, of all other ideas. If I could sum up my philosophy of ministry in one phrase it would be, 'Begin with Scripture'.

When you begin with Scripture, in the realm of decision making, you will be able to make your decisions on the basis of solid biblical precepts, commands and principles. The Bible will not tell you what house you are to buy, but it will frame that decision with financial, ministerial and family guidelines. It may not tell you to move to 334 South Grant Street, but it will present issues such as: Are your financial priorities biblical or are you thinking only of your comfort; how much can you truly afford; are you buying for prestige or in order to meet the needs of your family and better minister for the Lord; will this move be the best thing for your spouse, etc? It is biblical concepts such as these that enable us to make decisions that honour Christ.

Pray for wisdom (James 1:5-8). This passage in James is principally in the context of trials; many of the decisions we make are during just such times. James tells us that God will answer our prayer for wisdom, when asked in faith, but he does not say how. If wisdom is defined as the application of the knowledge of the Word of God, then perhaps the Lord opens our minds to the understanding of his truth in a unique way when we pray. We can't be certain of the methodology but we can be certain that God will answer. Again, we are not told that the Lord will specifically make the decision for us through some form of prompting, only that he will provide wisdom for making a wise decision.

Wise counsel. The Scriptures are replete with encouragement for us to seek the counsel of wise and godly people (Prov. 12:15; 13:10; 15:22; 20:18). Additionally, Paul tells believers that they should be involved in counselling one another (Rom. 15:14). The counsel of wise, godly and scripturally knowledgeable people is an important source for making wise decisions, but we must keep in mind that such counsel is not infallible. It is a piece but it does not solve the puzzle.

Circumstances and opportunity. The same can be said concerning these two. Circumstances and opportunities offer us options — options that should be carefully examined. But again these options are not obligatory mandates from God. Because we are offered a job in Indiana does not mean that we must take it. Because God has 'opened the door' for us to teach junior high boys does not mean we have to do so.

Desire. God often works through our desires. What is it that we want to do? is a good question to ponder. In 1 Timothy 3:1 Paul writes that those who desire to be elders desire a good thing. But carefully note, Paul did not tell Timothy to grab all who desire the office of elder and install them. Rather, he lays out for Timothy the requirements that an elder must meet (3:2-7; see also Titus 1:5-9).

This would be a good time to mention the 'call' to ministry. This is a controversial issue, and even some who would agree with the position I am presenting in this book want to cling to some concept of a call to ministry. So we need to take a careful look at what the Bible says on this subject.

The normal use of the term 'called' is in reference to salvation, 'God is faithful, through whom you were called into fellowship with His Son, Jesus Christ our Lord' (1 Cor. 1:9). Only three times in the New Testament is someone called to ministry: Paul is called to be an apostle (Rom. 1:1; 1 Cor. 1:1); Barnabas and Saul to go on their first missionary journey (Acts 13:2) and Paul to take the gospel to Macedonia (Acts 16:9-10). These three unique callings do not establish a norm. What about all the other ministers in the New Testament who did not receive such a call — how did they know they were to be elders (pastors) or missionaries or where they were to go? Since the Bible appears to be silent on the subject, just how does a person make a choice as to whether he should be in what we might call vocational ministry? I believe that the New Testament gives us some definite help here.

John Newton (author of the hymn 'Amazing Grace') offered some advice concerning a 'call to ministry' that I think was on the mark. He suggests these three tests for those considering the ministry: First is the test of desire — do you have 'a warm and earnest desire to be employed in this service?' This is in alignment with 1 Timothy 3:1, 'If a man aspires to the office of overseer, it is a fine work he desires to do.' The passage provides no information as the source of this desire — it just recognizes that an elder should aspire to the office.

Secondly, do you possess the necessary spiritual gifts and abilities for the office — 'There must in due season appear some competent sufficiency, gifts, knowledge and utterance. Surely, if the Lord sends a man to teach others, he will furnish him with the means.' This is supported clearly in the New Testament instruction on spiritual gifts (1 Cor. 12; Rom.12:3-8; Eph. 4:11-16; and 1 Peter 4:10-11).

Opportunity was Newton's third test.[1] We find throughout the Bible that God sovereignly provided opportunities for ministry when he saw fit.

To Newton's marks, I would add the necessary spiritual requirements as listed in 1 Timothy 3 and Titus 1. These lists contain mostly spiritual characteristics but also include the ability to 'exhort in sound doctrine and refute those who contradict' (Titus 1:9). In other words, they must be able to teach the Word and stand against and correct those who do not. If a man is not gifted to teach the Word, he should not consider the ministry.

Freedom. Surrounded by these principles, and others found within the New Testament, we are given freedom to make choices that we believe will glorify God (1 Cor. 10:31). Many Christians are uncomfortable with such freedom, having been taught that the perfect will of God could be found through some extra-biblical means. But the good news is that God, within biblical parameters, has given us the freedom and ability to make wise choices that honour him.

CHAPTER SIX

'BUT WHAT ABOUT?'

Earlier chapters explained that the subjective, mystical understanding of the Lord's leading through inner revelations, rather than through Scripture, is not biblically founded. This chapter addresses some of the questions that often arise on the subject.

Q. Many in the charismatic movement believe that God is speaking today through prophecies and words of knowledge. They insist that such revelation is not in contradiction to the written Word and that it should not be given equal status or added to Scripture. How does this charismatic view of revelation differ from the non-charismatic view of God speaking and leading through hunches and inner voices?

A. Not much if any. In essence, a charismatic theology of revelation has been adopted almost wholesale by the larger evangelical community. What is missed by both groups is that revelation from God, no matter what format or venue, is still revelation from God. It is not possible for God to give revelation that is not authoritative and demanding of obedience. All revelation from God carries the authority of Scripture. Now, it is true that God has not chosen to insert all his revelation onto the pages of the Bible. It is possible, for example, during biblical times that the Lord spoke to his servants but did not choose to include that conversation in the Scriptures. Nevertheless, whatever he said at those moments carried the full weight and authority of the written Word. Jesus said many things during his life on earth that were not recorded in the Bible, yet all he said carried the authority of God. Today many are claiming to hear from God, but what they are hearing, they say, does not have the status and significance of Scripture. This is logically impossible. Either God has spoken or he has not. If he has spoken, that message is as authoritative as Scripture. I agree with John MacArthur who wrote, 'God reserved divine revelation for special times, which were encompassed in the written Word, and since that time revelation has ceased.'[1]

Q. I believe that God is giving extra-biblical revelation today. My only problem is how to discern God's voice from my own or another source. How can I do so?

A. Henry and Richard Blackaby's book, *Hearing God's Voice*, was written largely to address this question, but even these foremost experts in the field failed miserably at a solution. They suggest that, to hear God's voice, faith is required,[2] as is the conviction that God speaks apart from Scripture.[3] We can expect new Christians,[4] they write, and those not in the habit of hearing from God, to be a bit disoriented for a while,[5] but hopefully that will all change and we will gradually come to recognize when God is speaking.[6] And 'the closer you get to God, the more easily you'll recognize his voice'.[7]

None of this is helpful. The problem is that this whole conversation is out of alignment with what we find in Scripture. First, virtually every time God spoke in biblical history the recipient had no doubt that he was hearing the voice of God — no matter what his spiritual condition or level of faith. With the exception of the child Samuel, virtually everyone, including unbelievers (e.g. Pharaoh, Balaam and Saul), immediately knew when God was speaking. Additionally, no formula or instruction is found in the Word to teach us how to discern God's voice. Learning to hear God's voice is simply not taught as a skill we must develop. The modern non-charistimatic, non-cessationist (those who believe that revelation is still being given today, mainly through inaudible means) have created a category of revelation not found in Scripture. They must now attempt to defend their view through experience because no biblical defence is possible.

It must be recognized that almost everyone is a cessationist of some sort. No one says, 'Anything goes'. But if we do not draw the line at Scripture there exist no criteria by which to determine where to draw the line. Had God intended revelation beyond the pages of the New Testament he would have provided us a means by which to discern his voice. Had God determined to change his mode of revelation from verbal communication to inner feelings and voices, we would have expected some notification of this change. We would have also expected some instructions by which we could decipher his message. He did none of these. We must therefore conclude that God did not choose to launch a unique form of communication after the closure of Scripture. The problems we are encountering today concerning God's leading go back to this fundamental issue.

Q. We are being told that God is speaking today, either through inner voices or words of prophecy, but that these messages may be partially from God and partially from our own thoughts. Of what value are these types of communications when we can't be certain what portion of them are actually the words of God?

A. Such supposed messages from God are of no value at all and may be of real danger. If we don't know what portion or part of a thought, dream or prophecy is from God or from some other source, how are we to discern what God is trying to say? If we believe that God is telling us to marry Suzy, move to Virginia, buy a commercial building and start a new business, but we also know that at least half of that message could be our own wishful thinking, how do we know which half to obey (remember: when God commands we must obey)? Again, a real problem at this point is that nothing in Scripture answers this question. When God spoke in the biblical record it was a complete and understandable message. No one wondered how much of what they just heard was their own imagination and how much was of God, nor is any formula given for discerning the difference. Non-cessationists have entered a shadowland for which there is no help biblically. They are left to their own devices.

Q. First Corinthians 14:29 mentions New Testament prophets who speak and then have others in the church body interpret what they had to say. What does this mean?

A. It must first be understood that the word 'prophecy' has a dual meaning. It can mean foretelling, as when prophecies revealed some future event, or forthtelling, as when a message from God concerning living for him is conveyed. This passage seems to be concerned with forthtelling, which itself comes in two varieties. On the one hand, there is the preaching or proclamation of the Scriptures, just as is done today. There was also divinely inspired forthtelling in which God gave a message of truth through certain individuals. This passage most likely is referencing both types of forthtelling.

It should be remembered that the church is built on the foundation of the apostles and prophets (Eph. 2:20), for it was these two types of gifted people who gave us the inspired Word of God. Hebrews 1:1 reads, 'God, after He spoke long ago to the fathers in the prophets in many portions and in many ways, in these last days has spoken to us in His Son…' Then later in chapter two, verses three and four, the author of Hebrews continues this thought by writing, 'How will we escape if we neglect so great a salvation? After it was at the first spoken through the Lord, it was confirmed to us by those who heard, God also testifying with them, both by signs and wonders and by various miracles and by gifts of the Holy Spirit according to His own will.' What is interesting is that this passage speaks of those who communicated the Word of God in the New Testament as a select group of people who heard these words from the Lord and were authenticated by miraculous signs.

In 2 Peter 3:2 we are told to 'remember the words spoken beforehand by the holy prophets and the commandment of the Lord and Savior spoken by your apostles'. Peter points to Old Testament prophets who gave us the inspired Old Testament corpus and to the apostles who gave us the inspired New Testament text. Every indication is that the New Testament revelation was delivered through the apostles and a few others closely associated with them (Mark, Luke, James, Jude and possibly the writer of Hebrews). John warns at the very closure of the New Testament that we are not to add to the prophecies of the book of Revelation (22:18, 19). Since the Revelation is the last book in the canon it is difficult to imagine how any additional prophecy today would not violate this warning.

When Paul gives the exhortation found in 1 Corinthians 14:29 he could be referring to both those who where preaching the already-revealed Scriptures and to those who were claiming an inspired word from the Lord. It should be remembered at that point the New Testament canon had not yet closed and God was still giving His inspired, authoritative Word. One of the problems the first century believers had to face was the issue of false apostles and prophets claiming divine authority. For this reason Paul spoke of false apostles (2 Cor. 11:13) and signs of a true apostle (2 Cor. 12:12). At Corinth there were those posing as divine spokesmen for God, even apostles. How were the Christians to test these claims? Paul said they were to 'pass judgment' on what these men claimed to have received from God. How were they to do that? First, by determining if these individuals had the signs of a true apostle. Next, they were to discern their message to see if it was sound. How were they to go about doing this? Were they to search for some subjective feeling of affirmation from the Holy Spirit? Nothing indicates that to be the case. Rather, as always, they were to 'examine the Scriptures... to see if these things were so' (Acts 17:11). In other words, even at a time when revelation was still being given, what people claimed to have heard from God had to pass the scrutiny of Scripture. Now that 'the faith [has been] once for all handed down to the saints' (Jude 3) and inspired prophecy has been declared ended (Rev. 22:18-19), there is no longer a need for further revelation to God's people.

Q. I often am impressed to witness or give a specific amount of money to someone. If God is not telling me to do these things then from where do these impressions come?

A. The source of our impressions, being subjective feelings, is impossible to identify. Surely we realize that unbelievers have impressions too; where do they come from? Trying to determine the source of impressions is futile, but most impressions simply come from our own thoughts. We see a person who needs Christ; we know the power and glory of the gospel; we long to tell others about the truth. What would be so strange about feeling an urge to tell folks about the Lord? Because we are impressed to share the gospel or anything else does not mean we have received extra-biblical communication from God. Impressions are impressions.

Q. What is the point of praying if the Lord is not going to speak to us during our time of prayer? Why even bother?

A. Until recently most Christians recognized prayer as our communication to God and the Scriptures as God's communication to us. But due to the influence of Henry Blackaby and many others, more and more believers expect God to speak to them during their time of prayer. Blackaby writes, 'In the Scriptures, prayer is often presented as a two-way conversation wherein people hear God respond to their prayers.... The key to God transforming us is not found in what we say when we pray but what we hear. As God speaks to us, we cannot remain unchanged.'[8] The biblical support for this type of understanding of prayer is scant. The most widely used New Testament text in its defence is Romans 8:26-27 about which Blackaby says, '[The Holy Spirit will] reveal the Father's thoughts and help believers know how to pray.'[9] But a careful reading of these verses in context does not render the Blackaby's interpretation. We are not being promised that the Holy Spirit will reveal to us the mind of God as we go to prayer. Rather, the promise is that the Holy

Spirit will intercede with the Father on our behalf so that our prayers are presented to the Father in such a way that they are in accordance with the will of God. This is necessary because we often 'do not know how to pray as we should' and the Spirit must conform our prayers to the plan of God.

It would be most helpful on this issue to study the prayers of the New Testament (e.g. Eph.1:15-23, 3:14-21; Col. 1:9-14; Phi. 1:9-11) . In these prayers there is no mention of praying a few words and then sitting back listening for the voice of God. New Testament prayers are the communication of the heart and mind of the believer to the Lord. They are not two-way communication. This concept is totally foreign to the New Testament. I am not denying that in the Bible God, on occasion, spoke to individuals as they were praying. But this is not the normal pattern given and, to make it the norm is to distort the expressed purpose of prayer, which is for us to speak to God.

Q. I often hear of someone entering into or being in the presence of the Lord. What does that mean and how can I know when I am in God's presence?

A. The New Testament teaches that Christians are indwelt by the Holy Spirit (1 Cor. 6:19) and therefore are constantly in the presence of the Lord. There is nothing that we can do to be more in the presence of God than we are right now. When a worship leader invites the audience to enter the presence of the Lord or someone asks the Lord to come into his presence, he misspeaks. In Hebrews 4:16, on the basis of the finished work of Christ, the child of God is invited to draw near to the throne of grace. That is, we now have direct access to God and we are encouraged to take advantage of that access in prayer. This does not mean we are nearer to the presence of God during prayer; it means because Christ is our High Priest we have the privilege of God's presence at all times and we can confidently approach him in prayer.

Those who speak of having experienced God's presence are usually referring to a subjective feeling that they have in which they believe they have encountered God in some unique way. Some very important questions should be directed to such experiences. First, what does the presence of God feel like? While someone might say that they felt peace or holiness or overwhelmed, nothing in the New Testament tells us what God feels like. Those who encountered God in a special way in the Scriptures were not describing feelings of God but direct tangible meetings with him. Such experiences with God were rare even in biblical times, even involving the most important characters in Scripture. The people of God did not live for these encounters nor did they expect them. Did this mean they lived hollow, empty, emotionally deprived lives? Not at all.

I am reminded of the men on the Emmaus road who did not recognize that they had been talking to Jesus until after Jesus disappeared. They immediately turned to one another and said, 'Were not our hearts burning within us while He was speaking to us on the road, while He was explaining the Scriptures to us' (Luke 24:32). Such experiences, in which our heart 'burns within us' as we are exposed to God's truth, should be common in the life of the believer. This does not mean we have entered the presence of God (we are already in the presence of God) but that our hearts have been touched by his truth. These moments should generate true passion for God, not because God's presence is nearer to us, but because our hearts have been drawn closer to him in love.

Q. If the evidence of the presence of the Holy Spirit is not a particular emotional experience then what is the evidence of the Holy Spirit in my life?

A. Biblically, the evidence of the Holy Spirit in our lives is not feelings but spiritual transformation. Two important passages, both often used out of context, help us here. Romans 8:14-16 speaks of the Holy Spirit leading in our lives, but the leading here is towards sanctification. It is through the Spirit's power that we are gaining victory over the deeds of the body (vv. 12-13). In Galatians 5:16-25 we recognize the presence of the Holy

Spirit by the spiritual fruit that he produces in our lives. Christ-likeness is the mark of the Holy Spirit, not a particular type of emotional encounter.

Q. Are you saying that God has no will or plan for my life? Wouldn't such a view be practical deism in which God created us, set certain things in motion, handed down some moral precepts then walked away and left us on our own?

A. Again, we must distinguish between God's sovereign will, his revealed (moral will) and his individual will. God sovereignly rules over all things. In his providence and omniscience the Lord has all things planned out according to his purpose and for his glory — and that includes his will for our lives. God's sovereign will is the secret things that belong to him, according to Deuteronomy 29:29a, and cannot be known to us until revealed in time. God's revealed or moral will is his general will for all people as recorded in Scripture. It is God's revealed will that belongs to us and is to be observed (Deut. 29:29b).

When speaking of God's individual will the proper question is not whether God has a sovereign plan known only to him for our lives. The answer to that question is yes. The real question people are asking when it comes to the **individual will** is, 'How can I know God's **sovereign will** for my life?' They want to know if God has given them a means whereby they can storm the gates of heaven and unlock the secret counsels of God. If so, what are those means? What I have tried to show is that Scripture gives no such formula; rather the Lord lays out for us principles and guidelines whereby we are able to make wise decisions which are in accordance with God's (revealed) will. As someone has said, 'The insistence of Jesus and Scripture was not on the importance of discovering the will of God, but always upon the necessity of doing it.'

The biblical picture is that God is vitally involved in our lives in ways that we cannot imagine, and in many cases will never know in this lifetime (Rom. 8:28). At this time we are walking 'by faith, not by sight' (2 Cor. 5:7).

CHAPTER 7

A SURVEY OF SCRIPTURE

I was recently handed the Fall 2005 catalogue of *Quaker Books*. The promo found in the catalogue for the book *Creeds and Quakers* reads like this:

> Quaker spiritual authority lies not in belief systems — in creeds — but in the direct communication between individual Friends and the Divine Spirit. All other forms of authority, 'be they written words [including Scripture, I would presume] steeple-house or a clerical hierarchy', cannot replace this direct communion.

This is historic Quaker theology in which the 'inner light' emanating from the Divine Spirit carries final authority, even over Scripture. While hotly denied by most, I believe that on a realistic basis much of evangelicalism is not only headed the same direction, but is there now. Few if any evangelicals, or even charismatics for that matter, would be as blatant as the Friends. Almost all would place final authority on Scripture when filling out their doctrinal statements, but when the rubber meets the road the final authority for many, as with the Quakers, rests not on the inscripturated Word of God, but on inner voices and subjective promptings. This is well illustrated in the writings of Henry Blackaby who has done more to promote subjective, mystical (non-classical) Christian living than any other modern non-charismatic leader. In a book co-authored with his son Richard, he writes,

Whenever God speaks, his Word becomes a north star for your life. It doesn't change. It is sure. As you accumulate a record of God speaking to you over the years, you will have a clear picture of where God has led you. This will give you powerful assurance as God continues to lead you in the future.[1]

This is a frightening statement when you realize that the Blackabys are not speaking about the Scriptures but of supposed private, nonverbal communication from God that is being given equal status with the Scriptures. Note the capitalization of 'Word' in reference to these extra-biblical messages from God. Also note that these messages take on the characteristics of Scripture as they become God's Word which guides us, gives us assurance of the future, and is even written down for later reference.[2]

The Blackabys are being consistent in recognizing where their view leads. In reality, they have adopted and popularized a theology which allows for additions to the Word of God. If one takes the Blackabys' position, this all makes perfect sense and is, in fact, inevitable. If God is specifically speaking to each of us, giving instructions on every consequential issue, we have to wonder what role Scripture plays? For some, the Bible becomes a dead book of ancient stories and staid theology. Once they master those things, they are ready to move on to the 'fresh' word of God being given today through inner voices within their souls. Under this scenario, Scripture becomes secondary at best and most likely unnecessary (except for basic doctrine). Soon we wake up to discover that we have embraced the Quaker's view of revelation and authority.

Some will ask, 'Isn't it true that almost all of God's children in Scripture heard from God directly? If this was the norm in the Bible, shouldn't we expect the same today? God has not gone mute, has he?'

First, because something happened in the Bible does not necessarily mean that it was meant to be normative for all times. God often did specific things for specific people at specific times that were not repeated, even in Scripture. Only with one person (Moses) did he speak 'face to face' as speaking to a friend

(Exod. 33:11; Deut. 34:10). Only at the hands of Moses, Elijah and Elisha did God perform great miracles in the Old Testament; only on one occasion did God deliver his Law; and so forth.

As to the issue of God speaking to almost everyone in the Scriptures, that is simply not true. The average believer in either Testament never heard a personal word from God, and even the majority of key players never heard the voice of God personally. When God did speak in Scripture it almost always dealt with the big picture of what God was doing in the outworking of his redemption program or the life of his people in general. You will search in vain to find God telling people what job to take, how many donkeys to buy, or what land to purchase — except as it was related to the bigger issue of God's dealings with his people.

The claim is made by some that the believers during biblical times heard the voice of God on a regular basis. The implication is that God personally spoke to and directed almost everyone who lived during the days that Scripture were being written — and did so all the time. And, if that is true, why should we not expect the same today? In response we need to take an objective survey of Scripture to see if this assertion can be substantiated. In this overview we will discount hearing the word of God through the prophets — God's appointed spokesmen before the closure of Scripture. We are looking for those who personally heard God's voice (or angels sent by him) either audibly or through inner words of promptings or impressions.

The first thing we find is literally thousands of lesser known personalities of which we hear nothing about this aspect of their lives. Neither Methuselah, nor Jabez, nor Jeshua the priest, nor countless others, heard the voice of God to our knowledge. While this is an argument from silence (for those on both sides of the debate) we should expect the biblical record to relay to us faithfully the normal life of the believer of that time. If the norm was for the common person to hear God speak regularly and personally we would expect a witness to this in Scripture. But such a record is not to be found. So we must turn our search to the major persons of biblical times.

The Old Testament

Below are some of the important characters found in the Old Testament who never heard directly from God as far as we know:

Caleb, Esther, Mordecai, Ruth, Joab, Hezekiah, Josiah, Jehosaphat, Jonathan, most of the judges, Ezra, Nehemiah, Shadrack, Meshach and Abed-nego (although they may have been comforted by the Son in the fire). In addition whole categories of key leaders never heard from God personally, including none of Jacob's sons except Joseph, none of the kings of Judah after Solomon, none of the judges except for Gideon, none of the returning exiles and none of David's mighty men or military leaders. This is just a sampling; many more could be cited.

There were of course several, usually important, individuals who did hear from God directly, or from an angelic representation. Besides the prophets we could list:

Noah and his sons (Gen. 6:13; 7:1; 8:15; 9:1,8,18)
Job (Job 38-42)
Abraham (16 times)
Abimelech (1 time) (Gen. 20:3)
Isaac (2 times) (Gen. 26:2, 24)
Rebekah (1 time) (Gen. 25:23)
Jacob (8 times) (Gen. 28:12,13; 31:11,13,14; 32:1, 24-
    32; 35:1; 35:10; 46:2-4)
Hagar (1 time) (Gen. 16:13)
Sarah (1 time) (Gen. 18:10-15) (She heard God talking
    to Abraham)
Pharaoh (1 time) (Gen. 41:25)
Laban (1 time) (Gen. 31:24)
Moses (at least 85 times)
Aaron (Exod. 4:27; 6:13; 12:1; Lev. 10:8; 11:1; 13:1;
    15:1; Num. 2:1; 4:1,17; 12:4; 18:1; 19:1; 20:12)
Miriam (1 time) (Num. 12:4)
Joshua (Deut. 31:23; Josh. 1:2-9; 3:7; 4:1, 15; 5:2,9,15;
    6:2; 7:10-15; 8:1, 18; 11:6; 20:1)

Gideon (2 times) (Judg. 6:14-36; 7:2-9)
Manoah and his wife (1 time) (Judg. 13)
Samuel (1 time before the beginning of his prophetic ministry) (1 Sam. 3:10-14)
David (1 Sam. 23:2, 10-12; 30:8; 2 Samuel 21; 5:19-25; 21:1)
Solomon (3 times) (1 Kings 3:5-14; 9:2-9; 11:11-13)
Simeon (1 time) (Luke 2:25)
Mary (1 time) (Luke 1:30)
Joseph (2 times) (Matt. 1:20; 2:13)
Zacharias (1 time) (Luke 1:13)
The Magi (1 time) (Matt. 2:12)
The Shepherds (1 time) (Luke 2:10)
Women at the Tomb (1 time) (Mark 16:6)

Beyond these few individuals, finding a non-prophetic individual in Scripture who heard directly from God becomes a difficult task. Some additional observations should be made. First, with a few exceptions, those cited above played extremely important roles in the outworking of God's program. Secondly, when God did speak, he did so in an audible voice or, on occasion, through a vision or dream. There is no reported account in which the Lord spoke through an inner, inaudible voice somewhere in the heart or mind of the individual. Next, these revelations from God are inevitably of profound significance, not just to the individual, but often to large numbers of others as well.

The contention that God spoke to almost everyone all the time, leading, guiding and directing, simply does not stand the test of careful study of the Scriptures. Even with those to whom God spoke, only with Noah, Abraham, Moses, Jacob, Aaron, Joshua, David and Solomon does God speak more than twice in their entire lifetimes. Additionally, the notion that God's revelation often came in a 'still small inner voice' is not warranted. Even the one occasion in which God did speak in a 'still small voice' to Elijah is often misunderstood. In 1 Kings 19:12-13 we find that Elijah hears a 'gentle blowing' of the wind. Out of that gentle wind came the 'voice' of God. The text does not actually say that it was a 'still small voice'. It says nothing at all about the intensity of the sound of the voice. But even if it was a quiet voice, it was still an audible voice. How many Christians, on the basis of misunderstanding of this passage, have claimed that they too have heard the voice of God? They claim to have heard an inner, nonaudible voice — just like Elijah. But Elijah heard no such thing. It was the voice of God — clear and distinct.

The New Testament

But what about the New Testament and especially the book of Acts? Isn't the evidence of God's direct guidance in the lives of church-age saints overwhelming? Actually, no. A detailed study of New Testament Scriptures does not reveal what many claim.

Virtually all of the New Testament accounts of God speaking and giving direct instruction are found in the book of Acts. This in itself is significant, but I will save that until later. If we give our attention to the book of Acts we find thirteen distinct times in which God spoke directly to individuals (two of these through angels): 8:26-29; 9:4, 10; 10:3, 11-16; 12:7-8; 13:2-4; 16:6,9-10; 18:9; 21:4, 11; 22:17-21; 23:11. The Lord used varied methods to communicate on these occasions including visions, angels, prophecy, and direct words from Jesus or the Holy Spirit. Of these thirteen revelations, eight of them were to two apostles (Paul and Peter). The other five were scattered among Philip, Annanias, Agabus, Cornelius and the church at Antioch.

A number of things stand out about these special words from the Lord. First, God takes the initiative each time. The recipients were not seeking revelations from the Lord, and on two occasions (Saul and Cornelius) unbelievers were on the receiving end of the message. Next, it should be noted that none of these individuals needed to learn a method of hearing God and, in every case, the hearers had no doubt that it was the Lord who was speaking. This is especially interesting in the case of Saul, an unbeliever at the time, who immediately addresses Jesus as 'Lord'. Also, in each case that we can discern, the message was given in an audible voice. There is no terminology such as 'I felt the Lord leading' or 'I had peace about what I was to do'. What God had to say was clear and beyond misunderstanding or misinterpretation.

Using just the book of Acts, we should immediately recognize a strong contrast between what was taking place there and what is being claimed today. In Acts we do not find every believer hearing from the Lord all the time about everything. Actually, we find six people and one congregation who heard from a member of the Trinity or an angel (two while still unsaved), and the things they heard were of great spiritual significance in the program of God. In Acts, no one had to learn how to hear God's voice nor was anyone led by hunches or promptings. The voice of God was unmistakable and his message was crystal clear. In Acts no one is encouraged or instructed to seek the voice of God; rather they were just going about their business when God intervened.

Acts is a book of happenings. It tells us what God did; it does not always explain why God did what he did nor does it necessarily set a norm for us today. This fact gets even more interesting when we leave Acts and begin to study the epistles. The epistles, unlike Acts, do not major on historical accounts, but instead focus on instructing the believer concerning how to live in the New Testament era. The silence concerning miraculous events and hearing the voice of God is almost deafening in the epistles. No one is called, instructed or urged to seek the voice of God. Instead, they (and we) are told to pay attention to Scripture (cp. 2 Tim. 3:15-4:4). Doctrine, truth and instruction, as found in the Old Testament and the apostles' teaching, are the bread and butter of the epistles. It appears to me that if the Lord had something better (or more) to offer beyond the Scriptures, he would have made it a point to say so in the epistles. Instead, he inspires Paul to write, 'Preach the Word'.

Fowler White represents my sentiments:

> The Bible gives us no reason to expect that God will speak to His children today apart from the Scriptures. Those who teach otherwise need to explain to God's children how these words 'freshly spoken from heaven' can be so necessary and strategic to God's highest

purposes for their lives when their Father does nothing to ensure that they will ever actually hear those words. Indeed, they must explain why this is not quenching the Spirit. Moreover, the promise of such guidance inevitably diverts attention from the Scriptures, particularly in the practical and pressing concerns of life. In the Bible the church hears God's true voice; in the Scriptures, we know that He is speaking His very words to us. Advocates of words 'freshly spoken from heaven' should beware: By diverting attention from the Scriptures, they quench the Spirit who is speaking therein.[3]

I believe our mandate today is this: rather than seek extra-biblical communication from God, we need to diligently learn how to handle the Word of Truth — in order that we might be 'approved by God as workmen who do not need to be ashamed' (2 Tim. 2:15). I like the way the English Puritan, Thomas Watson, said it, 'They who leave the light of the Word and follow the light within them, as some say, prefer the shining of the glow-worm before the sun.'[4]

CHAPTER 8

BIBLICAL GUIDANCE IN PRACTICE

The position I have taken throughout this book is one that I would call a full *sola Scriptura* understanding of the Christian life. This means that God speaks today exclusively through the authoritative, inspired Word which needs no supplementation from any other source. This is not to deny 'general revelation' from God's creation which tells us something of the power and glory of the Creator (Ps. 19:1-6; Rom. 1:20). But when it comes to 'specific revelation' we do not expect our Lord to speak to us apart from the Scriptures. His guidance is not to be sought in visions, dreams, angels or other supernatural manifestations. Nor are we to look inwardly for hunches, promptings, 'still small voices', or the peace of God. Even circumstances, opportunities, 'open doors', and good counsel, while of great help in our decision-making, are not authoritative. We are wise to carefully consider these outward matters but they do not carry the weight of Scripture nor do they constitute a mandate from God.

If we accept this *sola Scriptura* thesis, how do we go about 'finding' the specific will of God for our lives? We do so by examining the teachings of the Scriptures themselves. We can start by noting that there are a number of instances in the New Testament in which the Lord specifically states his will for us:

- It is God's will that we be filled with the Holy Spirit — 'So then do not be foolish, but understand what the will of the Lord is. And do not get drunk with wine, for that is dissipation, but be filled with the Spirit' (Eph. 5:17-18). At the moment of conversion *every* child of God is immediately indwelt (1 Cor. 6:19), baptized (1 Cor. 12:13), regenerated (Titus 3:5-6) and sealed by the Holy Spirit (Eph. 1:13; 4:30). These ministries of the Holy Spirit bring to the believer the unique presence of God, unite us to Christ and His body, create within us a new nature and secure our position in Christ. None of these is optional equipment for the Christian. The filling ministry of the Spirit, on the other hand, is not automatic, it is conditional. To be filled with the Spirit means to be controlled by him. When the believer is living in humble obedience to the Lord he is filled, or controlled, by the power of the Holy Spirit. It is the expressed will of God that we be filled with the Spirit.

- It is God's will that we be sanctified — 'For this is the will of God, your sanctification; that is, that you abstain from sexual immorality' (1 Thess. 4:3). The term 'sanctification' means 'to be set apart' and, when used in a Christian setting, takes on the connotation of being set apart for a holy purpose. In the immediate context of the First Thessalonians text the Lord is calling for moral purity. It is the expressed will of God that his people live morally pure lives.

- It is God's will that we be thankful — 'In everything give thanks; for this is God's will for you in Christ Jesus' (1 Thess. 5:18). Gratefulness seems to be contrary to our flesh and so is not a natural quality, yet God wants his children to be thankful. It is most instructive that in Ephesians 5:20 Paul lists giving of thanks as resulting from the filling of the Holy Spirit and Colossians 3:16 speaks of 'singing with thankfulness in your hearts to God' as springing from being indwelt by the word of Christ. Gratefulness is not to be humanly manufactured; it is a by-product of the control of the Spirit and the Word in our lives. It is the expressed will of God that his people be thankful.

- It is sometimes God's will that we suffer — 'For it is better, if God will it so, that you suffer for doing what is right rather than for doing what is wrong' (1 Peter 3:17). It is not always in the plan of God that we suffer for his sake but, when it is, we are to suffer because of our godly testimony, not because of sinful behaviour. It is sometimes the expressed will of God that we suffer for him.

These are, of course, general statements that are true for all Christians at all times — and this is not an exhaustive list. To these 'will of God' commands we could add all the revealed requirements, demands and mandates found in the Word which are applicable to the New Testament believer. Bottom line — we find the will of God through the careful study of the Word of God. This would include everything from a husband loving his wife as Christ loves the church (Eph. 5:25) to Christians not suing one another (1 Cor. 6:1-8) to the restoration of a fallen believer (Gal. 6:1-2).

Finding God's Will?

What we are discovering is that God has not hidden his will from us necessitating a secret formula to unravel his mysteries. His will for us is found right on the pages of Scripture ready to be plucked to the delight of all Spirit-indwelled children of God willing to read and apply the Divine revelation. The goal, as expressed in the New Testament, is not to find the will of God but to do the will of God. Since God wants you to do his will, be assured that he has not hidden it and then sent us on some kind of cosmic treasure hunt to find it. He is not daring us to discover the clues which will lead to his plan for our lives. Rather, his will is clearly imprinted on the pages of Scripture. It was to this end that Paul told Timothy to 'be diligent to present yourself approved to God as a workman who does not need to be ashamed, accurately handling the word of truth' (2 Tim. 2:15). Many are simply unwilling to do the 'diligent' work necessary to accurately handle the word of truth and are looking for shortcuts. The Lord does not call for shortcuts; instead 'diligence' is prescribed.

What would a *sola Scriptura* understanding of the will of God and decision-making look like in practice? Maybe the best way to approach this would be to use an actual example. Let's back up to my decision to speak in Brazil as mentioned earlier. As you will recall I was asked to go to Brazil for seventeen days to minister to Brazilian pastors at a retreat, present a number of seminars on contemporary trends facing the church today and preach at several churches. In addition, I would have the opportunity to observe the ministries of both Brazilians and missionaries and offer counsel.

Obviously, these are all good things — it would certainly seem to be the Lord's will to go. But offsetting the positive were a number of negatives. It would take hundreds of hours to prepare the materials needed for the trip, partly because my PowerPoint presentations and notes would all have to be translated into Portuguese — a huge task which I personally could not do. I would have to draw on a small army of helpers to accomplish such a huge task. On the other hand I am in a unique position in that a number of people in my church speak and write Portuguese (certainly unusual for a church in the cornfields of Illinois). Volunteers lined up to produce the materials and do the translation work — seemed like God at work, but there were other obstacles.

For one, I would have to be gone from my own church for two and a half weeks and miss three Sundays, something neither I nor the elders of the church find desirable. And what about all the other projects that I am involved in such as writing, counselling, preparing teaching materials and the like? While other staff members and elders could fill the pulpit and minister to the immediate needs of the people while I was gone, none of them could handle these other projects for me. I would come home to an almost insurmountable workload — and I would come home exhausted. There would also be a good chance that I would acquire some kind of exotic 'bug' while in Brazil, something I often manage to do when travelling abroad (at this I proved to be successful once again). Then there was the financial situation. This was an expensive trip and, as with most ministries of this nature, the expense would be all mine.

So, while a ministry in Brazil presented a wonderful opportunity, it offered many difficulties — the decision was not cut-and-dry. It certainly would have been nice if the Lord audibly told me what to do. Barring that, I could have used some reliable hunch or prompting. I would have been happy with just a little of the 'peace of God' guiding me, but as usual I was both at peace and simultaneously anxious over either decision. Examination of circumstances and 'open doors' led both ways and, as mentioned earlier, godly counsel was of little help. So what was I to do?

In the end, I chose to make the trip, but on what basis? God had not spoken to me either audibly or mystically. Peace was elusive as was good counsel. Doors were open in all directions. Obstacles were equally evident at every turn. Even Scripture contained no verses saying, 'Thou shalt (or shalt not) go to Brazil.' How could the right decision be made — one which would most honour God?

Biblical Decision Making

Actually that last question is misleading. I asked, 'How could the **right** decision be made — one which would most honour God?' That presupposes there is only one right decision that could have been made to bring God honour. But is that true? Had I chosen to stay home, attend to my local congregation, preached and taught the Word in the States, focused on my extended writing ministry and spent quality time with my family, would I not have made a decision that glorified God? Would I have disobeyed the Lord and thus have been living in rebellion (shades of Jonah) if I had taken this route? Many would say yes, but I believe the Bible says no.

Look for example at how decisions were made in the New Testament:

- Financial giving was to be done on the basis of the choice of the heart (2 Cor. 9:7).

- Travel to another country or town (except on the few occasions when God audibly stepped in) was left to the individual (1 Cor. 16:5-7; Acts 20:16).

- Consumption of various foods was determined by the conviction of the eater (Rom. 14:2-4; 1 Cor. 8).

- Observance, or non-observance, of special holy days was a personal decision — one not always shared by other godly people (Rom.14:5-9).

- Marriage, after proper obedience to biblical commands and principles, was left to the wishes of the individual (1 Cor. 7:39-40).

- Those in church leadership should aspire to the office (1 Tim. 3:1).

- Those in business, while leaving room for the sovereign will of God to the contrary, were free to pursue their business as they saw fit (James 4:13-17).

In none of these examples, and many more we could list, do we find the believer seeking the specific will of God. No hunches, promptings or experiences of inner peace come into play. These individuals went about their business obeying the revealed will of God, doing what they deemed to be the wisest and best for a given situation, always cognizant and open to the fact that God might change their plans. New Testament Christians did not always operate from a position of absolute certainty, nor did they seem to have the need to do so. It was not uncommon for Paul, for example, to take a course of action because he 'thought it was best' (1 Thess. 3:1), or because he 'thought it necessary' (Phil. 2:25), or 'if it is fitting' (1 Cor.16:4).

This was the typical decision-making process in the New Testament by godly people. As they lived in obedience to the revealed will of God, they made decisions based on the best information they had as they sought to honour God. In the end they made wise, informed choices according to their own desires, while they lived in conformity with the Word of God and always kept as their goal the glory of their Lord. At that point there is no evidence that they agonized over possibly being out of the will of God. They were in the will of God by virtue of their obedient lives. They, therefore, had the freedom to make wise, godly choices according to the best information that they had at their disposal. In any given situation a number of decisions could have been made, all of which equally honoured the Lord.

Let's plug all of this into my choice regarding the trip to Brazil. To the best of my knowledge I was living in the will of God by virtue of the fact that I was striving to live in obedience to Scripture. My life's passion is to bring glory to our Lord. Whether I stayed home or headed to Brazil would not change either of these things — I believed myself to be in the will of God as described by the Word. So I did not agonize over my status before God. Either decision, I believed, could and should bring honour to the Saviour. But I reasoned that I have spent virtually my entire life in the States. America has been the focus of almost all of my efforts in ministry — despite there being great needs in other places — needs the Lord has equipped me to meet. I had no pretence that my ministry in Brazil would be earth-shaking; still I knew that the Lord uses many different instruments, as weak as we might personally be, to accomplish his purposes. I believed I had something to contribute to the

Christians in Brazil. In addition, the church I pastor was healthy with a number of good leaders to superbly handle the ministry on the home front without me for a few weeks (actually much longer than that but I hate to admit it). The finances were in place and my work load could be managed if I would make good use of my time while travelling.

In the end I decided to go to Brazil because I wanted to go and because I believed it would be the best use of my time for the glory of God. Looking back I still believe it was the best choice. However, had I chosen to decline the trip, I could have done that for the glory of God as well. Either choice was a good one. Either choice was pleasing to God (2 Cor. 5:9). Neither choice would place me out of his will.

As we try to make decisions that honour God we should freely examine circumstances, feelings, logic, etc, but we can never conclude from such things that the Lord is definitely leading us in a particular way. The biblical picture is that of God's people making wise decisions based upon the clear commands and principles from the Scriptures. At the same time they were ever ready to bow before the will of a sovereign God who might at any time change their direction. Such Christians are not concerned about missing God's will because they are living in God's revealed will and they trust the Lord to take the initiative to make certain they are where He wants them to be. In the New Testament we are not told to seek God's will but to make wise decisions based upon biblical commands and principles. The understanding of these principles gives the child of God wonderful freedom and great confidence in their pursuit of lives that please their Lord.

CONFIDENCE IN THE WORD

My wife and I were having supper one evening in the home of friends. As the end of the meal a beautiful looking dessert was served. But as we dug in it quickly became apparent that the appearance was deceiving. The dessert looked wonderful but the taste just was not there. After some reflection it was determined that the sugar had been left out of the recipe. That missing ingredient made all the difference in the taste of the dessert.

While outwardly evangelicalism in much of the world appears robust and healthy, I believe there is a major ingredient missing in the lives of many Christians today. That missing ingredient is confidence in the sufficiency of the Word of God. The Scriptures are under attack. Of course, this is nothing new; we can trace such attacks to the Garden of Eden. What is new in evangelical circles is the package. Let's back up for a look at recent church history.

The theological battles that had been waged in Europe in the 1800s manifested themselves ultimately in the United States as well. In the 1920s and 30s differences between conservative and liberal churches came to a head in America. Out of that controversy came new denominations, fellowships, schools, missions, etc., which separated from those no longer believing in biblical Christianity. These organizations were founded by believers who desired to hold fast and 'contend earnestly for the faith' (Jude 3). One of the big problems at that time (as it is today) was developing a consensus concerning the essentials of the faith. That is, what doctrinal truths were absolutely necessary? What did all Christians who claimed to be orthodox believe and, conversely, what could be left to individual convictions? In other words, what was non-negotiable in the faith? A series of volumes, published originally in 1909 entitled *The Fundamentals for Today*, were an attempt to answer those questions. Written by some of the finest conservative scholars and church leaders of the day, *The Fundamentals* addressed the doctrines of Christology and soteriology, but almost one third of the essays concerned the reliability of Scripture. What emerged from this has become known as the Fundamentalist movement. A Fundamentalist was simply one who adhered to the fundamentals of the faith, primarily as described in *The Fundamentals*. One of those fundamentals was the belief in an infallible and inerrant Bible.

As time moved on, those who would become known as evangelicals split from Fundamentalism. Evangelicals still held to the fundamentals of the faith, but believed there was more room to compromise and work with those who denied some of the essentials. Of course, today there are many sub-groupings under these titles, but that is not our subject. Our point is that, by definition, all Fundamentalists and evangelicals supposedly adhere to the belief that the Bible is the only authoritative revelation from God to man, without error in the original, and is correct in all that it affirms.

While the Fundamentalist camp has continued to firmly hold this position, there has been considerable evidence of weakening on the evangelical side. For example, in 1976 Harold Lindsell, former editor of *Christianity Today* and typical evangelical, wrote a book called *The Battle for the Bible*. In this book, he documented the compromise taking place concerning biblical infallibility and inerrancy in such evangelical organizations as Fuller Seminary, the Southern Baptist Convention, and the Lutheran Church (Missouri Synod). The book was not well received. He followed it with *The Bible in the Balance* in an attempt to show the danger the evangelical world was facing because of its eroding view of the Scriptures. He wrote, 'Today an increasing number of evangelicals do not wish to make inerrancy a test for fellowship.'[1] His lament throughout the book was that evangelicalism was slowly losing its conviction in an inerrant Bible. Conversely, he believed that Fundamentalists were standing firm on the Scriptures.

Few heeded Lindsell's warning and, as a result, thirty years later it has become increasingly difficult to define an evangelical. Recently, in a futile effort to define the term, one journal resigned that an evangelical today is anyone who claims to be one. There are no longer any definitions. Lindsell suggested in 1979 that all Christians who wish to maintain an orthodox view of Scripture may want to return to the term 'fundamentalist' even with all of its negative connotations.[2] With this we happily agree if, by the term, we mean one who stands for the essentials of the faith including an inerrant and infallible Bible.

However, many who accept the Fundamentalist label (defined by its original meaning) have their problems in regard to the Scriptures as well. While they firmly stand for infallibility and inerrancy, as do conservative evangelicals, many have sadly compromised on sufficiency.

By the sufficiency of Scripture I mean that the Bible is adequate to guide us into all truth pertaining to life and godliness. Based upon such passages as 2 Peter 1:3; 2 Timothy 3:15-4:2 and Psalm 19, I believe the Scriptures alone (through the power of the Holy Spirit) are capable of teaching us how to live life, how to mature in godliness, how to handle problems and how to know truth. The Bible needs no help from the wisdom and experiences of men. Yet, the vast majority of both evangelicals and Fundamentalists believe the Scriptures are either inadequate or incomplete in communicating what the Christian needs to know in order to deal with the issues of life. Thus they believe that something in addition to Scripture is necessary.

A Biblical Example

There is nothing new about God's people believing that the Bible is insufficient to meet their needs. Colossians 2 describes a church during the New Testament era that felt it necessary to add several things to Scripture in order to move on to maturity. The church at Colossae apparently had come under the influence of the early stages of Gnosticism. Gnostics taught that certain individuals were privy to mystical sources of knowledge beyond the Scriptures. If one wanted to move on to maturity, according to the Gnostics, he had to tap into this extra-biblical knowledge through the methods that they taught. The Colossians, under this influence, were leaving behind the apostolic instruction concerning the Christian life (vv. 1-7) and were being deluded into adding at least five things to God's Word:

PHILOSOPHY

Colossians 2:8-15 warns of the danger of being taken captive through philosophy and empty deception. 'Philosophy' means the 'love of wisdom' and the book of Proverbs tells us that the love of wisdom is a worthy pursuit (Prov. 4:6). God does not oppose wisdom; He is against the wrong kind of wisdom. Paul warns of a pseudo-wisdom that can be identified by three characteristics:

- It is according to the traditions of men. That is, wisdom that comes from the mind of men, not the mind of God.

- It is according to the elementary principles of the world. This is likely a reference to the attempt to gain esoteric knowledge through mystical means, something the Gnostics loved (see v. 18).

- It is not according to Christ. True wisdom is found in Christ 'in whom are hidden all the treasures of wisdom and knowledge' (v. 3). The Colossians were searching in the wrong place for wisdom. What they were looking for was found in Christ, through the Word, not in the philosophies of men.

LEGALISM

Everyone thinks he knows what legalism is, and no one, including the Pharisees, ever thinks he is legalistic. Colossians 2:16-17 describes legalism as majoring on the minors. It is living for the shadows instead of the substance. It is the belief that keeping certain rules and rituals wins favour with God. These rules and rituals almost always are things that do not emerge directly from the Word. Therefore, the danger lies in the fact that we have added our own ideas to God's in order to mature in godliness. We, in essence, declare that God's Word is insufficient to instruct us on how to live life; we must therefore assist him.

ASCETICISM

Asceticism is based on a misunderstanding of our bodies. It is the idea that God will be impressed and we will become more holy if we deprive our bodies of even those things that are good. The major flaw, as Paul says, is that it is a 'self-made religion' and thus once again an addition to God's revelation (Col. 2:20-23).

PRAGMATISM

Pragmatism is not specifically mentioned in Colossians 2 but nevertheless permeates the whole passage. Pragmatism is the error of determining truth by what appears to work. If some method or concept seems successful, if people feel better, if they respond to the gospel or go to church more often, then it must be of God. Instead of the Word of God determining how we live and what we do, pragmatism steps in and rules.

MYSTICISM

Paul describes the dangers of mysticism in Colossians 2:18, 19. The Gnostics taught that a few elite had received the gift of direct revelation through the Holy Spirit. These moments of inspiration took place through visions, dreams, and encounters with angels.[3] This divided the church into two classes, the haves and the have-nots (the truly spiritual and the unspiritual).

The heart of modern day mystics' problems is found in these verses: they are basing their theology on experiences rather than on the foundation of Jesus Christ as found in his Word. The end result is that such people are 'defrauded'. They are missing out on true biblical living because of their beliefs.

TODAY

As happened at Colossae, many in the conservative evangelical and Fundamental ranks are subtly adjusting their view of the Scriptures. These individuals would defend to the death their belief in the inerrancy and infallibility of the Word, but have softened in the area of sufficiency.

When I speak of the sufficiency of the Bible, I mean that it alone is adequate to train us in godliness. Only the Word reveals God's truth for living. On the negative side, this naturally implies that nothing needs to be added to the Scriptures for us to know truth and live godly lives. Therefore, when anything, whether it is man's wisdom, personal experience, pragmatism, tradition, or direct revelation, is touted as a means of accomplishing these things, then biblical sufficiency has been denied. By this definition we find the conservative Christian landscape literally covered with those who claim to believe in the authority of Scripture, yet in practice deny it by their extra-biblical sources of obtaining truth and guidance.

But is biblical sufficiency biblical? Does the Word claim to be adequate? In reply, we are reminded of 2 Peter 1:3, 'Seeing that His divine power has granted to us everything pertaining to life and godliness, through the true knowledge of Him...' How is life and godliness obtained? It is accomplished through the true knowledge of Christ, which is found only in the Word. 2 Timothy 3:16,17 reminds us that the Scriptures are inspired by God and are profitable for teaching, reproof, correction, and training in righteousness. Why? In order that we might be adequately equipped for every good work. We have to wonder, if the Scriptures are adequate to equip us for **EVERY** good work, and if they are able to lead us to **EVERYTHING** pertaining to life and godliness, what else is needed? Why search beyond the Scriptures for the things that God says the Scriptures alone supply?

In our support of the doctrine of biblical sufficiency we can do more than proof-text. The whole thrust of Scripture implies that the Word alone is sufficient to teach us how to live life and find guidance. As a matter of fact, the burden of proof that something beyond the Scriptures (visions, man's wisdom, inner voices, tradition, etc.) is needed lies with those who doubt sufficiency. Note the view of God's Word as found in Psalm 19. We are told that it is:

- perfect and will restore the soul (v. 7)
- sure, making wise the simple (v. 7)
- right, rejoicing the heart (v. 8)
- pure, enlightening the eyes (v. 8)
- clean, enduring forever (v .9)
- true and righteous altogether (v. 9)
- more desirable than gold (v. 10)
- sweeter than honey (v. 10)

There is no hint here that the Word is inadequate to equip us for whatever life throws our way. As the psalmist praises the Scriptures he implies that there is no need for help from any outside source. This is the picture that we get throughout the entire Bible. Human wisdom, observations and experience add nothing to the Scriptures.

Mysticism, either in its classical or softer form, is one of the most subtle forces that undermine sufficiency in the evangelical church today. John MacArthur's definition of the often accepted evangelical form of mysticism is helpful, 'Mysticism looks to truth internally, weighing feeling, intuition, and other internal sensations more heavily than objective, observable, external data ... Its source of truth is spontaneous feeling rather than objective fact, or sound biblical interpretation.'[4]

Many of us dismiss the faulty view of revelation held by charismatics as unbiblical, but turn around and adopt a similar understanding for our own lives and ministries. I believe this to not only be inconsistent with, but an unavoidable denial of biblical authority and sufficiency.

NOTES

Introduction

1. Ruth A. Tucker, *God Talk* (Downers Grove, IL: IVP Books, 2005), p.70.

Chapter 1

1. http://www.orthodoxytoday.org/articles/YannarasPietism.php
2. See *Christian History,* vol. V, #2, 'Pietism, a Much Maligned Movement Re-Examined,' p.19.
3. Mark Noll, *Elwell Evangelical Dictionary* (http://mb-soft.com/believe/txc/pietism.htm), p. 2.
4. *Christian History,* vol. V, #2, p.15.
5. Arnold Dallimore, *George Whitefield* (The Banner of Truth Trust: London, 1970), pp.172-174.
6. As quoted by F. David Farnell, *The Master's Seminary Journal,* vol. 13, #1, 'How Views of Inspiration Have Impacted Synoptic Problem Discussions', p.46.
7. George Gallup Jr., *The Next American Spirituality* (Victor: Colorado Springs, 2000), p.15.
8. Ibid., p.30.
9. www.biblesociety.org/wr337/wr337.thmhA%70challenge
10. Ibid., p.32.
11. Ibid., p.29.
12. Ibid.
13. John H. Armstrong, General Editor, *The Compromised Church*, 'Church-o-Rama or Corporate Worship', Monte Wilson (Wheaton, Illinois: Crossway Books, 1998), p.67.
14. Ibid., p.68.

15. *Christianity Today*, September 2005, p.61.

Chapter 2

1. Alistair Begg, *What Angels Wish They Knew* (Chicago: Moody Press, 1998), p.13.
2. Henry Blackaby, *Experiencing God: How to Live the Full Adventure of Knowing and doing the Will of God* (Tennessee: Broadman and Holman Publisher, 1994), p.88.
3. D. A. Carson, *The Gagging of God* (Grand Rapids: Zondervan, 1996), p.506.
4. Donald S. Whitney, 'Unity of Doctrine and Devotion', in *The Compromised Church*, ed. John H. Armstrong (Wheaton, IL.: Crossway Books, 1998), p.246.
5. D. Martyn Lloyd-Jones, *Fellowship with God* (Wheaton, IL: Crossway Books, 1993), p.95.
6. Sinclair B. Ferguson, 'The Evangelical Ministry: the Puritan Contribution', in *The Compromised Church*, ed. John H. Armstrong (Wheaton, IL.: Crossway Books, 1998), p.272.
7. Udo W. Middelmann, *The Market Driven Church* (Wheaton, IL: Crossway Books, 2004), p.61.
8. Elaine Pagels, *The Gnostic Gospels* (New York: Vintage Books, 1981), pp.49, 139-142, 163-166.
9. Jack Deere, 'Vineyard Position Paper #2', p.15.
10. Wayne Grudem, *The Gift of Prophecy in the New Testament and Today* (Wheaton, IL.: Crossway Books, 1988), pp.120-121.
11. Ibid., p.110.
12. David Wells, *God in the Wasteland* (Grand Rapids: William B. Eerdmans, 1994), p.109.
13. John H. Armstrong, ed., *The Compromised Church*, 'The Evangelical Ministry: a Tragic Loss' (Wheaton, IL.: Crossway Books, 1998), p.272.
14. R. Fowler White, 'Does God Speak Today Apart from the Bible' in *The Coming Evangelical Crisis*, ed. John H. Armstrong (Wheaton, IL.: Crossway Books, 1996), p.79.
15. Jack Deere, *Surprised by the Voice of God* (Grand Rapids: Zondervan, 1996), pp. 283-384.

Chapter 3

1. Kenneth Silverman, *The Life and Times of Cotton Mather* (New York: Harper & Row, 1984), p.173.
2. Ibid., pp.173-190.
3. Garry Friesen, *Decision Making and the Will of God* (Portland, Oregon: Multnomah Press, 1983), p.35.
4. Ibid.
5. See Revelation 21:14 which strongly implies that the inner circle of the apostles of the Lamb is limited to twelve. The other individuals mentioned in the New Testament as apostles (e.g. Barnabas), I believe were apostles (or sent ones) of the church and were not on the same level as the Twelve.
6. While Waltke's book *Finding the Will of God, a Pagan Notion?* has a number of insightful comments I nevertheless found it overall disappointing with Waltke often supporting the very things that he set out to disprove.
7. Bruce K. Waltke, *Finding the Will of God, a Pagan Notion?* (Grand Rapids: William B. Eerdmans, 1995), p.11.

Chapter 4

1. Dave Swavely, *Decisions, Decisions* (Phillipsburg, New Jersey: P&R Publishing, 2003), p.65.
2. As quoted in Swavely, pp.30-31.
3. Garry Friesen, p.131.
4. Don Matzat, *The Lord Told Me, I Think* (Eugene, Oregon: Harvest House, 1996), p.64.
5. Garry Friesen, p.98.

Chapter 5

1. John Newton, *Leadership,* vol. XI, #3, 'How Do I Know I Am Called', pp.55-57.

Chapter 6

1. John MacArthur, www.biblebb.com/files/MAC/NEWREV.
HTM
2. Blackaby, pp.52-53.
3. Ibid., p.213.
4. Ibid., p.257.
5. Ibid., p.214.
6. Ibid., p.235.
7. Ibid., p.210.
8. Ibid., pp.34, 122.
9. Ibid., p.37 (see also pp.116, 124, 137).

Chapter 7

1. Henry and Richard Blackaby, Hearing God's Voice (Broadman & Holman: Nashville, 2002), p.230.
2. Ibid., pp.227, 229, 230, 241.
3. Fowler White, 'Does God Speak Today Apart from the Bible?', in The Coming Evangelical Crisis, ed. John H. Armstrong (Chicago: Moody Press, 1996), p.87.
4. Don Kistler, ed., The Puritan Pulpit: Thomas Watson (Soli Deo Gloria Publications, 2004), p.141.

Conclusion

1. Harold Lindsell, The Bible in the Balance (Grand Rapids: Zondervan, 1979), p.303.
2. Ibid., p.320.
3. Elaine Pagels, The Gnostic Gospels (New York: Vintage Books, 1979), pp.49, 139-142, 163-166.
4. John MacArthur, Our Sufficiency in Christ (Dallas: Word Publishing, 1991), p.32.